MW00378598

In case of loss, please return to:

_____

_____

_____

_____

As a reward: $ _____

Birds and Bees

A CONVERSATION ABOUT GOD, SEX, AND SEXUALITY

Gregg Matte

Published by LifeWay Press®
© 2012 Matte Ministries

No part of this work may be reproduced or transmitted in any form or by any means, electronic or mechanical, including photocopying and recording, or by any information storage or retrieval system, except as may be expressly permitted in writing by the publisher. Requests for permission should be addressed in writing to LifeWay Press®, One LifeWay Plaza, Nashville, TN 37234-0135.

ISBN: 978-1-4158-7235-2
Item: 005474745

Dewey Decimal Classification Number: 306.7
Subject Heading: SEX \ POP CULTURE \ SEX (PSYCHOLOGY)

Printed in the United States of America.

Young Adult Ministry Publishing
LifeWay Church Resources
One LifeWay Plaza
Nashville, Tennessee 37234-0135

We believe that the Bible has God for its author; salvation for its end; and truth, without any mixture of error, for its matter and that all Scripture is totally true and trustworthy. To review LifeWay's doctrinal guideline, please visit *www.lifeway.com/doctrinalguideline.*

From the Holy Bible, New International Version, copyright © 1973, 1978, 1984 by International Bible Society. Used by permission.

Cover design by The Visual Republic

TABLE OF CONTENTS

ICON LEGEND

 Things to
listen to

 Things
to watch

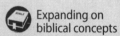 Expanding on
biblical concepts

Fun facts and useful
tidbits of information

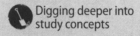 Digging deeper into
study concepts

 Available tools for
group leaders

 On the
Web

MEET THE AUTHOR
GREGG MATTE

My name is Gregg Matte. I was born and raised in Houston, Texas, and I trusted Christ as my Savior at the age of 16. Since then, God has done an extraordinary work in me and through me. In 1989, as a Texas A&M sophomore, my roommates and I started a small Bible study named Breakaway in our apartment. By the power of prayer, Breakaway exploded, reaching more than 4,000 students each week. It's still going strong today with even more students and is making a great impact in collegiate lives (*breakawayministries.org*).

In 2004, God called me to become the pastor of Houston's First Baptist Church. Our church has grown tremendously and is impacting the world as never before. I hold a marketing degree from Texas A&M and a Master of Christian Education from Southwestern Baptist Theological Seminary. I have been able to write a couple of books before this one, *Finding God's Will* and *I AM Changes Who i Am*. Most importantly I'm married to Kelly, the most wonderful woman in the world. She was definitely worth the wait (see my notes to her in Session 6). We have two children: Greyson and Valerie. What a blessing they both are—and a lot of fun!

I wrote *Birds and Bees* because the beauty and blessing of sex has become tainted since, well, the moment after Adam and Eve ate the fruit. Thankfully, God has not left us alone to figure things out. The Bible is filled with guidance for sex. My hope and prayer is that this study will help you heal and grow in your understanding of God's plan for sex and sexuality.

As part of my passion to rescue the vulnerable from sex trade, a portion of the royalties from this study will go to As Our Own. This ministry rescues and adopts little girls from the red-light districts in India. To find out more, go to *asourown.org*.

SPECIAL THANKS FROM GREGG

To LifeWay and the entire Threads team, I'm grateful for your trust and hard work. Thanks to Dennis Perry, my youth minister and father in the ministry. You have lead me well on these topics. To Ralph Borde and As Our Own, what an encouragement to partner with you to rescue children from the darkest places in India into His glorious light. Houston's First Baptist Church, it's a blessing and a joy to be your pastor. And to Kelly, my beautiful bride, I'm blessed beyond measure to be your husband!

God has a plan

If you've flown on a commercial airplane in the past decade, you probably had to watch a flight attendant demonstrate how to buckle and unbuckle a seat belt. I'll be honest: I don't have a lot of positive feelings about those demonstrations.

That's not to say I have anything against flight attendants—I think they do a great job, generally speaking. It's just that I've been buckling and unbuckling seat belts for years, and there are few experiences in life more tedious than being forced to endure an explanation of something you already know how to do.

That being the case, let's get something straight off the bat: You already know how to have sex. Maybe you've already had sex. If you're a virgin, chances are good that you've seen a sex scene during a movie or TV show. Maybe you've encountered pornography. At the very least, you probably had to endure some kind of lecture about sexual intercourse during health class in middle school.

For those reasons and more, this study isn't about "the birds and the bees" in the sense of an awkward conversation you may or may not have had with your parents when you were a kid. I'm not going to spend time discussing what goes where during the act of sex. (I'm not going to explain where babies come from, either.)

Rather, this study is about the deeper issues connected with sex and sexuality. It's about the fundamental needs and longings that have made sex such a foundational element of the human experience. Best of all, it's a chance to engage in a mature, practical conversation about those needs and longings in a way that applies to your specific situation.

TWO PRINCIPLES

In order to help you make the most of that conversation, I've framed the different sessions of this study around two main principles.

The first is that sex and sexuality are incredibly complicated topics. They involve a number of different layers and connections—physical, of course, but also emotional, social, and even spiritual. As such, a discussion about sex and sexuality forces us to examine our core identities as human beings, including gender and sexual orientation. It also helps us find answers to questions like *Who am I?* and *Why do I have these desires?*

In addition, thinking through these topics helps us discover the ways we've been influenced by our culture and past experiences. It gives us a chance to identify the wounds we've received, and hopefully start the healing process. It also gives us a chance to correct any false beliefs we've picked up, and to move forward with a better understanding of our needs and the needs of others.

The second issue around which I've framed this study is that God has given us a lot of advice about sex and sexuality through His Word. In fact, the Bible serves as both a blueprint for God's original design when it comes to sex and an instruction manual with practical guidelines for living out that design in our day-to-day lives.

THE BIBLE SERVES AS BOTH A BLUEPRINT FOR GOD'S ORIGINAL DESIGN WHEN IT COMES TO SEX AND AN INSTRUCTION MANUAL WITH PRACTICAL GUIDELINES FOR LIVING OUT THAT DESIGN IN OUR DAY-TO-DAY LIVES.

I've used 1 Thessalonians 4:1-8 as the primary text for this study, and we'll dig deeply into what God said through the apostle Paul in those verses. We'll also look at several other passages in Scripture to be sure that our conversation on sex and sexuality is profoundly impacted by God's Word.

THREE AUDIENCES

Maybe right now you're wondering: *Is this study for me? Does it have anything worthwhile to say to someone in my situation?* After all, a topic like "sex and sexuality" is fairly broad. And even if we restrict it to God's views on sex and sexuality, there's still a lot of ground to cover—a lot of different directions the content could go.

Let me save you a little time (and skimming) by revealing the three types of people I had in mind when I wrote this study.

First, if you're single and not currently involved in a serious relationship, I wrote this study for you. I spent many years as a bachelor in search of my wife, so I know how it feels to wonder if you'll ever meet the right person. Even if you aren't actively looking for a spouse, this study will help you face the pressures and challenges that come with "singles life" in today's culture.

Second, if you're single but in a serious relationship, I wrote this study for you. Dating relationships can be simultaneously exciting and terrifying, and those feelings only intensify when you add a physical connection to the mix. Participating in this conversation will help you set a practical, biblical plan for enjoying and evaluating your current relationship.

THE PUBLIC ASPECT OF OUR CULTURE'S VERSION OF SEX IS LESS THAN GOD INTENDED. WHILE IT'S POSSIBLY PASSIONATE, IT'S IMPOSSIBLY PLEASING TO US OR TO THE LORD.

Third, if you're married, especially recently married, I wrote this study for you. I understand that you want to have fulfilling experiences with sex. You want to have fun and memorable experiences with your spouse, but you also want your physical relationship to open the door to deep and lasting intimacy—something that transcends "intercourse" and results in two people becoming one. Participating in this study with your spouse will help you move in that direction.

In this study we will see the truth that God, the Author of all that is good, has blessed humanity with the joy of sexual intimacy. It's uncomfortable to talk about because this topic is personal; it brings up insecurities, guilt, joy, sadness, fear, uncertainty, and a host of other emotions. Wherever you fall on the spectrum, these pages are not an attempt to embarrass or rebuke you but to focus you on God's intentions, as revealed in His Word.

One of the culprits of our skewed understanding of sex is the amount of exposure we've had to it. From childhood, we've seen TV programs, Web sites, and gossip magazines at the grocery checkout line guiding our views. Countless love scenes on the silver screen to gossip in the halls of high school have slowly shaped us. Through limitless TV and movies we've come to believe intimacy is found on the third date—or even the first. It appears to peak when feelings brim over as the soundtrack plays to the crescendo. Yet the blessing of the Lord is "sexual intimacy," meaning intimate, between two people. Have you ever heard it called "sexual publicly"? The public aspect of our culture's version of sex is less than God intended. While it's possibly passionate, it's impossibly pleasing to us or to the Lord.

So let's reclaim intimacy for God's glory and our satisfaction. Let's believe the truth, not the lie. Let's turn the pages of God's Word instead of allowing screens to bring us wonder. Let's long for marriage not lust for mating. There's more to God's plan, so much more.

Are you ready to join in this conversation? I hope so. It's my prayer that you'll dive into this study with an open heart and mind so that your experiences with sex can be as sweet and passionate and tender and powerful as God always intended them to be.

The first time I heard about sex, I was an elementary school kid with strawberry blond hair and freckles across my nose. I was young, but focused, listening to someone I considered a wise and eminent sage— a fifth-grader. With a know-it-all attitude, he told me about the birds and the bees. I responded forcefully to his claims: "My parents never did that!"

Of course, as time went by my innocent eyes were pried open by TV sitcoms and movies I was too young to see (but saw anyway). I even remember receiving an NFL cheerleaders' calendar as a gift from a relative. The inadequately-clothed ladies had autographed their photos. One even signed her photo, "Remember room 101." Who signs autographs suggesting they have shared a hotel room? I was an 8-year-old! You should've seen my dad squirm when I asked, "What does room 101 mean?"

A few years too late my mom sat me down for "the talk" and that was it. My education on one of the most complex, dangerous, and wonderful subjects of the human experience consisted of a big kid in the neighborhood, a few episodes of "Three's Company," a cheerleader pin-up, and "the talk." There was no mention of waiting, true intimacy, possible pitfalls, or God Himself.

I remember thinking, *There's gotta be more!* Even at a young age, I realized I hadn't been adequately prepared for love and sex. I just didn't know where to look for the knowledge I craved.

How were you introduced to the topic of sex?

What's been most helpful in your "sexual education" over the years?

What was left out of your early conversations? What was added that shouldn't have been?

 In a Rand Corporation study, researchers discovered that 40 percent of adolescents had had intercourse before talking to their parents about safe sex, birth control, and STDs.[1]

SESSION ONE BIRDS AND BEES

IT'S TIME FOR A GROWN-UP CONVERSATION

Whenever I take a trip, I try to pack my suitcase well. I try to bring everything I may need in order to live and operate in a strange place. If I forget something important—or if I waste valuable space with useless stuff—I may be in big trouble.

In the real world, many people are relying on poorly packed suitcases as they journey through understanding sex. That's how I felt as a younger person. In fact, sometimes it seemed like my suitcase was just about empty. Maybe that's how you're feeling now.

Unfortunately, because we live in a sex-saturated culture, our suitcases don't stay empty for very long. Unless we fill them with the truth about God's design for sex and sexuality, our suitcases will become piled full of junk from the world around us as the years go by. For example, most people's suitcases contain whispered, uneducated discussions they had with friends when they were kids. Most people carry images they picked up from billboards and magazines. They carry snippets from movies and TV shows, and the lyrics from hundreds of songs.

Others have stuffed their suitcases with their own choices and actions. They've experimented with sex (or have dived head-first into a sexual lifestyle). They've built their statuses and self-worth on a foundation of physical attraction. They've indulged in premarital sexual relations, cohabitation, extra-marital affairs, open marriages, or pornography.

Others have been forced to carry around the choices and actions of those around them; they've been abused, raped, betrayed, or abandoned. Many, including myself, have seen their parents choose divorce over marriage.

Take a quiet moment to "unpack" your suitcase. For your eyes only, write down the decisions or actions, made by others or yourself, that are dragging you down. Whisper a prayer as well.

Given all that baggage, it's time for us to put down our suitcases and have an honest conversation. We need to open up and talk about what we've been dragging around all these years. We need a chance to lift up our doubts and have our questions answered. Unfortunately, there's not a lot of opportunity for that kind of conversation in today's culture.

Watch the *Birds and Bees* video for Session 1, available at *threadsmedia.com/birdsandbees*.

SEX AND CULTURE

Not that our culture avoids the topic of sex—far from it. Society uses a megaphone to shout its views about sex in all directions. This is especially true of the advertising industry. For example, how often have you heard the term "sex sells"?

Here's the problem: What we hear from advertising megaphones concentrates on the physical aspects of sex. It's void of the elements that make our sexual experiences powerful—commitment, trust, emotional intimacy, and so on. As a result, sex is reduced to variations of animal instinct and lustful desire. Just as bad, what we hear from our culture's megaphone is often juvenile and crass. Sex is connected with cheap arousal and crude humor.

Take a minute to review what messages you receive from the entertainment and advertising industries. Place a check mark next to each scenario you've seen in movies, TV shows, and commercials during the past month:

> ❏ **A person being idolized because of frequent sexual conquests**
> ❏ **A person labeled a "loser" because of a lack of sexual experience**
> ❏ **Sex being used to show that people have fallen in love**
> ❏ **Sex being used to sell a product or experience**
> ❏ **Adultery referenced as a joke**
> ❏ **Homosexuality praised**
> ❏ **Other scenarios not listed above**

My goal is to highlight the "lowest common denominator" approach our culture takes toward sex. It's almost as though entertainment and advertising executives view consumers as middle-school kids who never grew up. We need to move away from this mind-set if we want to have a grown-up conversation about sex and sexuality.

If our culture is a poor venue for honest discussion, where should we talk openly about the birds and the bees?

The best option is to have a lifelong conversation about sex within the context of a loving, committed family—ideally a conversation that starts young and provides a place for questions to be freely asked and honestly answered. If you had that kind of experience growing up, you're way ahead of the curve. You've been blessed.

Unfortunately, that's not the case for most people. I've talked with thousands of young adults over the last decade, and most of them are still looking for a mature, godly perspective on sex and sexuality. They're still searching for answers.

....

 Sexuality (noun): the feelings, thoughts, and behaviors associated with being a certain gender, being attracted to someone, loving, being in relationships, intimacy, and so on.

What did your parent(s) do well in regard to talking about sex and sexuality?

What would you do differently if you were the parent?

Believe it or not, the next best place to find those answers is within the local church.

SEX AND THE CHURCH

I'm not saying you need to seek answers to your sex-related questions within a church building, necessarily. There's a lot to be said for engaging deeper discussions in a setting where you feel most comfortable. But if you're going to talk about sex and sexuality in a way that's beneficial and productive, you need to find a community of people who are seeking to understand and follow God's design for those issues, too. And it's important that you find a community of people who value safety, empathy, and the power of forgiveness—in short, people who understand grace.

In my mind, the best place to find those qualities and that kind of community is the local church.

Maybe you disagree. Maybe you read that last paragraph and thought, *Whoa! You've never been to my church.* Maybe the idea of connecting "church" and "sex" makes you feel uncomfortable or even angry. If so, I can see where you're coming from. For decades, many churches have addressed the issues surrounding sex and sexuality by saying "don't": *Don't* have sex before marriage. *Don't* do anything with another person that might lead to sex before marriage. *Don't* dress provocatively. *Don't* look at pornography. Those are true statements, but the conversation shouldn't end there. So much more needs to be said.

How do you react to the "don't" statements above? Why do you think that's your initial reaction?

 The average age for one's first sexual experience is 15 to 19 years old—with generally younger ages for women than for men, especially in developing countries.[2]

What's missing when churches only communicate by saying "don't"?

Churches can't be ashamed to talk about sex because no one else in our society is ashamed to talk about it. And the ones talking most about sex only emphasize the physical elements and feelings involved—not God's plan.

God created us as sexual creatures. Our desires are from Him not against Him. But it takes biblical teaching and the Holy Spirit's power to walk in the best and right direction. It requires more than will power to honor God sexually; it has to be transformational power. We've allowed, knowingly and unknowingly, for the wrong to overshadow the right.

And unfortunately, the church has kept quiet when it should be the loudest to speak.

Why do you think the church is often afraid to discuss sex?

How does your church handle it?

More importantly, Christians can't afford to remain quiet about sex because we've been given the truth about those issues. We've been given the Bible, which is God's Word. Scripture has a ton to say about God's intentions and design for sex.

GOD'S WORD
I'll repeat that: The Bible has *a ton* to say about sex and sexuality. Numerous verses and whole sections of Scripture reference those topics—including Song of Songs, an entire book focused on sexual experiences, expressions, and emotions.

That much content can be overwhelming. So, for the purposes of this study, we're going to focus primarily on one section of Scripture from the apostle Paul:

 Jesus selected the apostle Paul to take the gospel to the non-Jewish people of his day. Paul is credited with authoring 13 books in the New Testament. You can find an extended biography on him in the Book of Acts.

"Finally, brothers, we instructed you how to live in order to please God, as in fact you are living. Now we ask you and urge you in the Lord Jesus to do this more and more. For you know what instructions we gave you by the authority of the Lord Jesus.

"It is God's will that you should be sanctified: that you should avoid sexual immorality; that each of you should learn to control his own body in a way that is holy and honorable, not in passionate lust like the heathen, who do not know God; and that in this matter no one should wrong his brother or take advantage of him. The Lord will punish men for all such sins, as we have already told you and warned you. For God did not call us to be impure, but to live a holy life. Therefore, he who rejects this instruction does not reject man but God, who gives you his Holy Spirit." (1 Thessalonians 4:1-8).

Re-read this passage and underline words and phrases that strike you as meaningful.

Consider memorizing this passage of Scripture throughout this study. If you're up for it, write out verse 1 below.

Now re-write verse 1 in your own words.

We'll explore other Scripture passages, of course, but this text will serve as our rudder and sail while we navigate some potentially stormy waters. It's a helpful summary of God's design for sex and sexuality. With that in mind, take a closer look at the beginning of verse 3: "For this is God's will." I can't overemphasize how important those words are. The apostle Paul wrote this entire passage of Scripture, but these aren't "just" his opinions. There's more going on.

For more on understanding God's will, check out author Gregg Matte's book, *Finding God's Will: Seek Him, Know Him, Take the Next Step* (Regal, 2010).

What we find here isn't good advice or the latest claim from a self-help manual. Rather, these verses contain "God's will" for sex and sexuality. They are commands that came directly from "the Lord Jesus" (v. 2). They carry His authority. They aren't the opinions of the kid down the street but of God in His holiness, love, and power. That's great news! That's a wonderful reality!

God invented sex. He has a will for sex. He has a plan for sexual orientation. Those things didn't spin out from creation by mistake or cosmic accident. God intentionally designed us as sexual beings. He has a distinct purpose—and He didn't keep that purpose to Himself. He told us about it in His Word. In other words, we don't have to figure things out on our own. Thank goodness (and thank God).

Before you read further, how would you describe God's will for sex and sexuality from what you've previously learned about His Word?

How do you respond to the statement that "God invented sex"?

GOD'S WILL

Of course, just because the Bible contains God's will about a topic doesn't mean we always follow His will.

Even as Christians, there are times when our ignorance or disobedience leads us to figure things out on our own. Or we put our faith in setting up systems based on prevention—on building fences. But even properly fenced sheep still need a shepherd to lead them toward greener pastures. The fences are important, but they're incomplete. They're not enough.

As a result, there have been some mixed messages from God's people in regard to His will for sex and sexuality. There have been churches and individual Christians who, from time to time, contribute to the discussion in a way that actually causes confusion rather than clarity.

 One study of sex on TV found that 70 percent of shows contained some form of sexual content.[3]

Mixed Messages

For example, conversations within the church about sex and sexuality have, at times, become focused on the avoidance of consequences. As I've said, well-meaning people, pastors, and parents (like me) often use *don't* as a primary theme when they talk about sex. *Don't* have sex before marriage because you'll get pregnant. *Don't* have sex before marriage because you'll get a disease. *Don't* have sex before marriage because you'll develop a bad reputation.

Such a message is all about avoiding consequences instead of honoring God. As a result, many people have come to believe that if they can avoid the consequences connected with sexual activities, their actions really aren't that bad. People have grown up with the idea that birth control/condoms will take care of everything—that they should follow their urges as long as they can do so without other people finding out.

That's not what God intended. The goal of the gospel is not to manage our sin, but to defeat it and to find life. Jesus' death on the cross calls us to the "more" of abundant life— not just to keeping consequences at bay.

Instead of *don't*, our conversations about sex and sexuality should be framed by *do*. *Do* honor the Lord. *Do* walk in purity. *Do* discover the best God has for you and wait until you're ready to receive it. Let's state what we're for rather than only what we're against. God is always on offense. He doesn't need to play defense because He knows our "yes" to Him produces a "no" to sin.

Growing up, what messages did you hear from churches on the connection between sex and consequences?

What messages did you hear from the culture?

One message we sometimes hear is abstinence solves everything. As long as you're not having sex, you're OK. That's a great start, but there are soul issues at stake as well as physical ones.

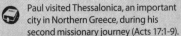 Paul visited Thessalonica, an important city in Northern Greece, during his second missionary journey (Acts 17:1-9).

The world says: "All sexual desires are good. Have sex when you want and with whomever you want." Churches have sometimes responded by saying the opposite: "Most sexual desires are bad. Have nothing to do with anything sexual until you're married." Here's the problem: Both of those messages only concentrate on the physical elements of sex. Both of those messages reduce sex to a physical act and ignore the deeper elements of sexual experiences. As a result, both messages are shallow, juvenile, and unhelpful.

Don't get me wrong: I believe that choosing abstinence is godly and virtuous. It's God's plan for us to steward and cherish our bodies until marriage. But it's important for us to choose abstinence for the right reasons. Simply avoiding sex doesn't mean you're operating according to God's plan. You can be a virgin and still be drowning in lust. You can be a virgin and still use your body to attract attention from others. You can be a virgin and still judge people in your heart and treat them cruelly when their preferences and actions are different than yours. That's not what God intended either.

The Original Design
So here's the million-dollar question: What *did* God intend for sex?

How would you answer this question?

We'll find the answer in 1 Thessalonians 4, but I want to start with some background information. That text is part of a letter Paul wrote to the church located in Thessalonica, and he used the first three chapters to offer personal greetings and historical review. Discussing his thankfulness for the Thessalonian Christians, he reminded them of his ministry in their town, and how concerned he was for the suffering and persecution they were experiencing.

Then, in chapter 4, Paul got down to business. He wrote a series of instructions and exhortations for the Thessalonians on how to live as followers of God. Verses 3-8 are instructions for sex and sexuality. Verses 9-10 deal with brotherly love. Verses 11-12 have to do with orderly living. Notice the motivation behind all of these instructions:

> **"Finally, brothers, we instructed you how to live in order to please God, as in fact you are living. Now we ask you and urge you in the Lord Jesus to do this more and more" (1 Thessalonians 4:1).**

 Listen to "The Birds and the Bees" by Dean Martin and "Like Wildflowers" by Rosie Thomas from the *Birds and Bees* playlist, available for purchase at *threadsmedia.com/birdsandbees*.

Paul wrote his instructions to help the Thessalonians "please God." Specifically, he wanted them to view sex and sexuality as opportunities to walk as followers of God and please Him.

When Paul lived with the Thessalonians, he taught them the basics of living as Christians. Once he left to plant churches in other areas, the Thessalonians tried to live according to Paul's teachings. They had made progress as new converts despite their lack of teaching. So Paul wrote 1 Thessalonians in order to provide further instructions for pursuing holiness and pleasing God.

To put it simply, then, sex is about pleasing God. And a mature view of sex begins with a desire to follow Him—not just to follow the rules or avoid consequences.

It's been that way since the beginning, which we can see in Genesis 1:

> **"So God created man in his own image, in the image of God he created him; male and female he created them.**
>
> **"God blessed them and said to them, 'Be fruitful and increase in number; fill the earth and subdue it. Rule over the fish of the sea and the birds of the air and over every living creature that moves on the ground.' . . . God saw all that he had made, and it was very good. And there was evening, and there was morning—the sixth day" (vv. 27-28,31).**

Just to make sure we're all on the same page, that command "be fruitful [and] multiply" refers to sex. Adam and Eve were created as sexual beings. Their union was part of God's design, and "it was very good." It pleased God.

Circle the adjectives in the verses from Genesis 1 above. What do you notice about the connections between them?

Does sex still honor God today? Why or why not?

 Ancient Semitic hospitality customs made Lot responsible for his visitors' safety while under his roof—no matter the cost.

 The Sodomites were also guilty of pride, arrogance, oppression of the poor, and "detestable things" (Ezekiel 16:49-50).

Like everything else in the world, however, sex was distorted when sin entered the picture just a couple chapters later. People drifted away from God's original design. Instead of viewing sex as pleasing God, they did as they pleased.

Actually, people didn't just "drift" away from God's plan for sex and sexuality. They dove off a cliff in their rebellion against God's design. For example, we only need to flip from Genesis 1 to Genesis 19 to read of the homosexuality and promiscuity in the city of Sodom:

> **"Before they had gone to bed, all the men from every part of the city of Sodom—both young and old—surrounded the house. They called to Lot, 'Where are the men who came to you tonight? Bring them out to us so that we can have sex with them.' Lot went outside to meet them and shut the door behind him and said, 'No, my friends. Don't do this wicked thing. Look, I have two daughters who have never slept with a man. Let me bring them out to you, and you can do what you like with them. But don't do anything to these men, for they have come under the protection of my roof'" (Genesis 19:4-8).**

Eden to Sodom is a big jump. Humanity went from God's blessing in a garden paradise to debauchery in the city streets.

Circle the adjectives in the text from Genesis 19. What do you notice about the connections between them?

How do the adjectives in Genesis 19 compare with the adjectives you circled from Genesis 1?

Fast-forward through thousands of years of distorted attitudes and practices, and you'll understand why Paul had to write the opening section of 1 Thessalonians 4. He wanted the members of that young church to understand God's original design for sex and sexuality so that they could honor God through their obedience.

 "'Teacher, which is the greatest commandment in the Law?' Jesus replied: 'Love the Lord your God with all your heart and with all your soul and with all your mind'" (Matthew 22:36-37).

GOD, SEX, AND US

Fast-forward another 2,000 years, and the same is true of today's culture. The same is true of you and me. We've drifted away from God's intentions, and we need to gain a better understanding of God's plan for sex and sexuality if we want to glorify Him. We need to return to God's design for sex if we want to experience a sexual relationship in its fullest measure—something beyond a merely physical connection.

I hope you have a lot of questions about that process. Questions like:

• What exactly is God's design for sex and sexuality?

• How far is too far when it comes to physical intimacy before marriage?

• What about homosexuality and other issues connected with sexual identity?

• What if someone has made mistakes in the past?

• What does the Bible say about divorce?

• How do I handle lust?

• What does it mean to honor God with my sex life?

We're going to address those questions throughout the remaining sessions of this study, all of them. Just be patient, as one session builds upon the other.

For now, however, the most important thing I want you to remember and reflect on is that sex begins and ends with pleasing and honoring God. Sex was created by God to glorify Him. Therefore, if we want to experience the full measure of what God intended for sex, we start by pursuing Jesus. If we aspire to a mature, helpful understanding of sexuality and everything that entails, we need to start by loving God.

If you're married, start by loving God. Realize that's where true fulfillment begins. Sex is far more than a physical act; it includes emotions, spirit, and trust. Then, take the love of Christ you've experienced and share it with your spouse. (More on that in Session 6.)

If you're single and you're wondering how to handle sexual desires with seemingly no place to go, start by pursuing Jesus. Then allow Jesus to lead you down the path He has in store for your future—whatever that path may be.

God is the Creator of sex. He's the One who gave it to us, and if we miss that fact, we miss everything. The purpose behind our sexuality, single or married, is to please Him. It's to be in love with Him and satisfied with Him—and that is good.

APPLY TO LIFE

> **CONNECT:** Whether you're single or married, try to get together this week with a married person you respect—preferably someone at least a little older than you. Talk with that person about his or her overall story, marriage, and opinions about the primary purposes of sex and sexuality.

> **STUDY:** Work on memorizing 1 Thessalonians 4:1-8 over the course of this study. This week, start with verses 1-2: "Finally, brothers, we instructed you how to live in order to please God, as in fact you are living. Now we ask you and urge you in the Lord Jesus to do this more and more. For you know what instructions we gave you by the authority of the Lord Jesus."

> **LISTEN:** Purchase "The Birds and the Bees" by Dean Martin and "Like Wildflowers" by Rosie Thomas (see the playlist at *threadsmedia.com/birdsandbees*). Add these to your regular mix of music throughout the week so that you'll be reminded to continue thinking about God's plan for sex and sexuality.

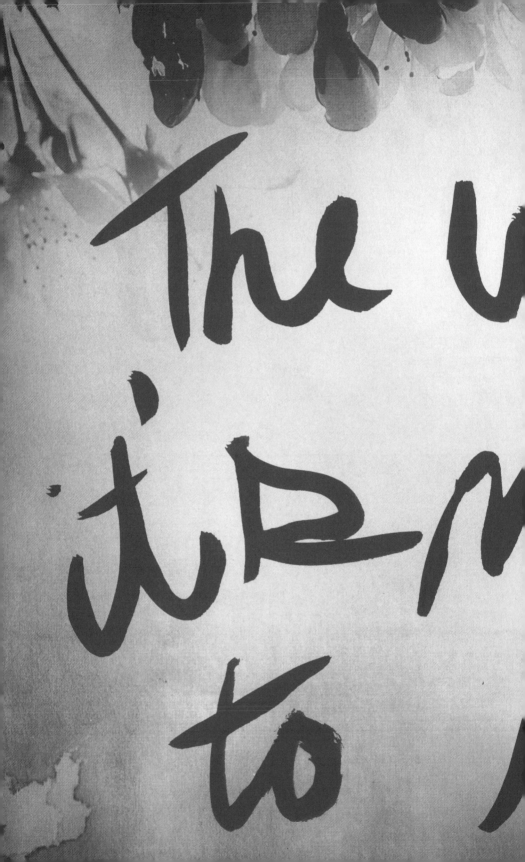

oay

meant

r

2

Some things in life are so important they demand a predetermined plan—things like emergency evacuation routes, weddings, or the first few plays of the Super Bowl. My college roommate would quote his father whenever we dashed into a project unprepared: "If you fail to plan, you plan to fail." Every time he mimicked his dad's words, I heard in them a deeper voice dripping with wisdom. It's true: Without plans we end up grasping at straws.

Sure, there are times to just go where the wind blows. I've often dreamed of arriving at the airport and picking a city from the "Destinations" screen. But whimsical vacations are markedly different than real, day-to-day life. The decision's importance, possible pain, or intended joy determines the depth of planning the experience requires.

Even the word *plan* strikes different chords within different people. Those who love calendars are "amen-ing" me for talking about plans, while those who prefer to hit "shuffle" on their playlists are thinking, *Loosen up.* Touché to both groups. Yet we can agree that the critical things of life require thought and preparation. Great lives don't just happen; they are intentional.

When have you been forced to go through an important situation or event without a plan? What happened?

What events or experiences in life are so important that they require a prearranged plan?

Intentional living means establishing goals and outlining objectives for how those goals will be achieved. One of the benefits of planning is to uncover and answer questions. And the uncovering of deeper questions leads to the uncovering of deeper answers. Planning forces us to evaluate where we currently are and where we want to be. That's good, because today's sexual views lack emotional depth, the result of a lack of godly intentions.

THE PLAN FOR SEX
As I mentioned in Session 1, God hasn't left us in the lurch when it comes to the birds and the bees. Our Creator understands the importance of our relationships with the opposite sex. He has a plan for sex and sexuality, and God communicated that plan to us through His Word. In fact, He started communicating His plan in the Bible's second chapter.

 Watch the *Birds and Bees* video for Session 2, available at *threadsmedia.com/birdsandbees*.

 Alan Lakein, personal time management author, is attributed with Lakein's Law on prioritizing and failing to plan.

"Then the LORD God made a woman from the rib he had taken out of the man, and he brought her to the man. The man said:

"This is now bone of my bones
and flesh of my flesh;
she shall be called 'woman,'
for she was taken out of man.

"For this reason a man will leave his father and mother and be united to his wife, and they will become one flesh" (Genesis 2:22-24).

The plan God has established is not complicated; it has two basic steps, but those steps are tremendously profound.

First, God's creation of human beings included the blessing of two separate genders— men and women. As frustrating and confusing as it may be when one gender strives to understand the other, it's a wonderful gift from God designed to mold us and fine-tune us by chipping away at our selfishness. The differences between genders were divinely designated and blessed. They're part of the plan.

Second, God intended for one man and one woman to leave their existing families and become "united" in marriage, to form a new family. This spiritual and physical union is about far more than just mating. It's not one animal choosing another animal instinctively. Rather, the calling of marriage is far higher. It's two people made in God's image listening to His direction and discovering how to give Him glory. Wow! That's the black velvet upon which the diamond of physical union should be seen.

Marriage is a vulnerable step of faith involving leaving one's family and making a lifelong commitment to a spouse. To "leave" and then "cleave" to another person means stepping away from the known and into the unknown. This union is emotional, conversational, financial, and ultimately physical based within a wonderful act of faith—in yourself and in the other person. The importance of the decision to enter into a marriage dictates the need for an intentional plan and process. Otherwise, the relationship can quickly derail or crack with foundational issues that were never properly addressed.

Within the context of marriage, God has intended for husband and wife to be joined together in such a powerful way that they become "one flesh." This is the beautiful and godly blueprint from which sex is intended to operate. What used to be two becomes one in God's eyes. We usually think of this in terms of physical intimacy, but it's much more. It's oneness at the depths of the soul that expresses itself in a physical way.

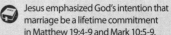 Jesus emphasized God's intention that marriage be a lifetime commitment in Matthew 19:4-9 and Mark 10:5-9.

What are your initial reactions to God's plan for sex?

How does God's plan compare to what you've been taught throughout your life?

Again, God's original intentions were not complicated. His plan was simple, elegant, and effective. But after the fall, life, love, and earth became distorted by sin. People began to move away from God's design in every way, including sexually. Now we live thousands of years from the original template. Centuries of men and women have marred the impression God set forth with Adam and Eve.

All of Scripture seeks to remind us about God's plan—and to inform us of the pain we cause others and ourselves when we deviate from it. Thankfully, we still have God's Spirit and Word to guide us back to His plan and help us live it out.

Proverbs 5:15-20 is a good example in regard to wedded love and intimacy:

> **"Drink water from your own cistern, running water from your own well. Should your springs overflow in the streets, your streams of water in the public squares? Let them be yours alone, never to be shared with strangers. May your fountain be blessed, and may you rejoice in the wife of your youth. A loving doe, a graceful deer—may her breasts satisfy you always, may you ever be captivated by her love. Why be captivated, my son, by an adulteress? Why embrace the bosom of another man's wife?"**

Many New Testament authors wrote to congregations from cultures outside of traditional Judaism. This highlighted the need to explain God's plan for sex and sexuality—and to interpret His plan in light of specific struggles or distortions present within those cultures. That's what the apostle Paul was doing in our central text from 1 Thessalonians 4. The Thessalonians needed major help dealing with sex in a godly way.

So God not only created a plan for sex and sexuality before the fig leaves of the Garden of Eden, but He spent thousands of years re-emphasizing that plan throughout the Scriptures. (For examples, see the story of Abraham and Sarah in the Book of Genesis, the Song of Songs, and the Book of Hosea.) The reason He went to all that effort is because the physical union of a man and woman is paramount in importance.

....

 New Testament churches like Corinth and Ephesus needed direction. They received letters helping them think through the issues of their time.

Make a quick list of the first five words that come to mind when you think of God's plan for sex and sexuality.

What Scripture correlates with the words you chose?

What repeated themes or patterns do you notice within those words or verses?

We are sexual beings, which means sex and sexuality are major elements of the human experience. They impact us at the core of who we are and who we were made to be. Sex is an incredibly complex issue, which means we have to face incredibly complex problems and conversations within our culture today.

I've been in ministry for more than 20 years, and in that time I've spoken to countless individuals. Through it all, I've seen far too many people drift into harmful attitudes and experiences when it comes to sex. Their lack of understanding resulted in bad decisions. Or they knew the truth but chose otherwise. Or they just put their heads in the sand to avoid the issues out of fear.

Failing to understand God's trustworthy intentions leads to humanity's failing inventions. Regardless of your age, embracing the intentions of God is the key to understanding the path He has laid out for sex and sexuality. God has created us with the intention of truly enjoying the birds and bees, not for the guilt, shame, and other wounds associated with misuse of His gift. Therefore, we need to align ourselves with the plan that God—the One who created sex *and* who created you and me—has already set in place.

My goal for the rest of this session is to help you discover the greatness of God's plan. I want to highlight some of the key elements of His will so that we may maintain a clear picture of God's design for sex and sexuality.

TWO WORDS
The first step toward following God's plan is to gain a proper perspective. Possessing the right attitudes about sex leads to taking the right actions. In 1 Thessalonians 4, Paul helps us move in God's direction by encouraging us to concentrate on two words: *holy* and *honorable*.

 Listen to "Come Thou Fount of Every Blessing" by Sufjan Stevens and "What Is" by Anna Vandas from the *Birds and Bees* playlist, available for purchase at *threadsmedia.com/birdsandbees*.

> "It is God's will that you should be sanctified: that you should avoid sexual immorality; that each of you should learn to control his own body in a way that is *holy and honorable,* not in passionate lust like the heathen, who do not know God" (vv. 3-5, emphasis added).

I like the way Paul simplified the issue for his readers. He could have said, "Each of you should learn to control his own body by creating and following a bunch of rules." He could have written out a long list of what they could do, what they couldn't do, what they should wear, what they shouldn't wear, and so on.

Thankfully, he didn't do that. Instead of creating rules, Paul lifted up our sexuality as holy and honorable. We'll reap a lot of benefits if we can wrap our minds around those two words.

What rules have you heard communicated by Christians when it comes to sex and sexuality? (We can agree that many of them are helpful.)

Jot down the first words or images that come to your mind when you read the words *holy* and *honorable*.

Holy

Here's how the dictionary defines *holy:* "specially recognized as or declared sacred by religious use or authority; consecrated."[1] In the Bible, if something was described as holy, it was set apart (or separated) from its surroundings. It was different.

The temple is a great example of something that was holy. In ancient Israel, the temple was located in Jerusalem. It was the heart of the city in many ways, but it was also separated from the rest of the city. People worked and socialized in the streets and buildings around the temple. They bought and sold goods of all kinds. They lived and loved and fought and reconciled.

But the temple was different. The temple was where people went to worship God. It's where they went to offer sacrifices and make atonement for their sin. It was separated from the rest of the city. It was holy.

Even within the temple, there was an inner chamber called the most holy place—the holy of holies—where God's presence dwelt. This area was so sacred, so holy, that only

---

 The Bible has much to say about holiness:
Leviticus 16; Romans 12:1-2; 1 Corinthians 1:2;
3:16-17; 1 Peter 1:15-16; and Revelation 4–5.

SESSION TWO BIRDS AND BEES

the high priest of the Israelites could enter it, and he was only allowed to do so once every year in order to make atonement for the sins of himself and of the people (Hebrews 9:7). The consequence of ignoring the holiness of that room was devastating:

> "The LORD said to Moses: 'Tell your brother Aaron not to come whenever he chooses into the Most Holy Place behind the curtain in front of the atonement cover on the ark, or else he will die, because I appear in the cloud over the atonement cover'" (Leviticus 16:2).

How do you react to that verse? What does it communicate about God's holiness?

What other people, places, and things are described as holy in Scripture?

Now, keeping in mind what we know about the temple, look at what Paul wrote in 1 Corinthians:

> "Flee from sexual immorality. All other sins a man commits are outside his body, but he who sins sexually sins against his own body. Do you not know that your body is a temple of the Holy Spirit, who is in you, whom you have received from God? You are not your own; you were bought at a price. Therefore honor God with your body" (1 Corinthians 6:18-20).

Notice how Paul communicates a difference between sex and other physical acts. "All other sins" that we commit have an effect outside of our bodies, but sexual immorality impacts us in a more personal way. And we can infer the reverse, as well—that following God's plan for sex and sexuality will be especially fulfilling for us.

Do you agree that sexual sins have a more personal impact than "all other sins"? If so, how?

Sex is to be holy. It's not a "run of the mill" physical act like riding a bicycle or eating a sandwich. It's different. It's set apart. Therefore, we need to treat it with the holiness it deserves.

 On the Day of Atonement, only the high priest was allowed to enter the inner sanctuary of the temple. He made reconciling sacrifices for the sins of the entire nation (see Leviticus 16:16-28).

That's what Paul communicated in 1 Thessalonians 4. He wanted his readers to set themselves apart from the motives, ideas, and values found in the world—found in people "who do not know God" (v. 5). In other words, Paul wanted them to be pure. He was urging them to behave in a way that was unstained by the world around them. The importance of this message in the culture of Paul's day was vast; the Thessalonian people were driven by their various urges and desires. They were steered by "passionate lust" (v. 5), which led to "sexual immorality" (v. 3). In other words, most people did whatever they wanted to do in order to gain instant gratification.

We can say the same about our culture. The world tells us that sex exists as a means for us to gratify ourselves, quickly and without commitment. We can incorrectly believe our value is based on appearance and our bodies are tools for gaining attraction and attention.

Where have you seen these messages communicated within our culture?

What other messages does our culture communicate about sex and sexuality? How do they differ from God's message?

The message of purity is different. Purity says that sex is a means of glorifying God. Purity says that my value is based on who I am inside—who God created me to be—and that my body is to be offered as a gift to my spouse alone.

I know it sounds weird to say that sex is a means of glorifying God. Just putting "sex" and "God" in the same sentence feels like tripping over a rock. It sounds awkward. This clumsiness is the result of putting an earthly view on a heavenly gift. Our post-Eden thoughts reflect on a pre-Eden gift. But proper thinking leads to proper living. Realizing sex is to be held in holiness and honor leads us to our holy and honorable God. All of life is a gift to be given back to Him, including our most intimate thoughts and actions.

Another prevailing notion in our culture is that impurity produces excitement. Commercials, billboards, and magazines continuously claim that the route to passion is doing whatever you want with whomever you want. They falsely portray marriage as tedious, redundant, and boring against the flair of unrestrained sexual expression. Such a notion may work for a 30-second commercial, but it won't work for 30 years of matrimony. It's a 30-second lie with 30 years of consequences.

 God's first commandment to Adam and Eve in the garden was for them to "be fruitful and increase in number . . . " (Genesis 1:28).

In reality, true passion only comes from true purity. Purity is the source of passion, and the greater the purity in your life and love for God, the greater passion you'll experience in physical intimacy in marriage.

Purity needs to be protected in our lives. Even more, it needs to be cultivated. Purity grows as a fine garden, tended as a mother cares for a child and protected as a soldier defends the king. We nurture purity by remembering that sex is holy.

Honorable
The second word Paul uses is *honorable*. Here's the dictionary definition: "being of high rank, dignity, or distinction; noble, illustrious, or distinguished."[2] When something is honorable, it's highly valued; it's not flippantly viewed or experienced.

What kinds of things are labeled as honorable in today's culture? In church culture?

Write down any instances you can find of things being labeled as honorable in the Bible.

When my wife, Kelly, and I began dating, we experienced the joy of gift giving. First was the gift of food. I would take her to dinner and she would bake a dozen cookies to say thanks. Then we graduated to flowers and cards on the right holidays. As the relationship grew, the gifts followed suit.

One of the most special nights of my life came when Kelly gave me an antique Bible. It was a huge coffee table-type Bible dated 1775. I remember holding that amazing book in my hands, awed that it predated the U.S. Constitution. With each reverent turn of a page, we wondered who had read these exact verses and touched these pages over the centuries.

One question wouldn't leave me, so I asked: "How did you pay for this?" I knew student teaching at an elementary school didn't provide enough income for gifts like a 1775 Bible. Her words touched my heart and affirmed her love for me: "Gregg, you didn't know it, but I got a job cleaning a family's house. I've been earning money for the last six months to pay for this Bible."

Far from the days when a dozen cookies were the right gift, she had literally scrubbed someone else's floors and washed another person's dirty dishes to bless me with one of the most meaningful presents I've ever received. To this day I treasure that Bible and have it on display in my office.

Our trust, conversation, and love had grown—and so had our gifts. That night was also the first time we told each other "I love you." When I look back on that evening, I'm so satisfied by the combination of our growing expressions of love with our growing gifts of love, both verbal and tangible.

If Kelly had shown up on our first date with an antique Bible, I would have run for the hills! But as the relationship grew, it made sense that the value of our gifts grew, as well. After that Bible, the next gift I gave Kelly was a diamond ring. She was to be mine forever.

What's the best gift you've ever received?

What made that gift so special?

There's a sensible progression in that story—it's almost instinctive. We naturally offer our most valuable gifts to the people we care about the most. According to God's design, the progression doesn't end with an engagement ring.

After a woman commits to love and respect a man within a marriage relationship, God's plan calls for her to give her most precious possession to her husband: her body. After a man commits to love and protect a woman within a marriage relationship, God's plan calls for him to give his body away to his wife.

> **"The wife's body does not belong to her alone but also to her husband. In the same way, the husband's body does not belong to him alone but also to his wife" (1 Corinthians 7:4).**

Can you imagine if I'd offered Kelly an engagement ring on our first date? Bad move, right? But I have to ask: Why are so many people willing to give away their bodies sexually when they are only financially ready to give flowers or candy? To do so is neither holy nor honorable. The gift is disproportionate to the relationship.

Look again at 1 Thessalonians 4:3-5:

> "It is God's will that you should be sanctified: that you should avoid sexual immorality; that each of you should learn to control his own body in a way that is holy and honorable, not in passionate lust like the heathen, who do not know God."

According to God's plan, sex is honorable. Sex is to be highly valued. It isn't casual, dirty, unnatural, embarrassing, shameful, scarring, or scary. It's a wonderful part of His creation to bring pleasure and to further creation within the marriage bed. God has lifted sex up to a high and holy level—not to prevent us from attaining the standard, but to make sure we truly respect and appreciate it.

Is it difficult for you to view sex as God-honoring? Explain.

Sex is the most significant act that can occur between two human beings. There's no other interaction in which we're dressed the same! Sounds funny, but it's more important than you may think.

Earlier in this session we explored Genesis 2:22-24 as a summary of God's plan for sex and sexuality. Look what God said in verse 25:

> "The man and his wife were both naked, and they felt no shame."

Lacking shame combined with nudity is significant and rare. Adam and Eve lived together as husband and wife, and there were no barriers between them—nothing to make them feel ashamed. But then sin entered the picture and distorted everything, including the relationship between Adam and Eve. We can see it in Genesis 3:

> "When the woman saw that the fruit of the tree was good for food and pleasing to the eye, and also desirable for gaining wisdom, she took some and ate it. She also gave some to her husband, who was with her, and he ate it. Then the eyes of both of them were opened, and they realized they were naked; *so they sewed fig leaves together and made coverings for themselves*" (vv. 6-7, emphasis added).

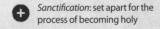

Sanctification: set apart for the process of becoming holy

The very first action Adam and Eve took after their sin was to cover themselves with clothing, and we've been doing the same thing ever since. Even our most elegant and expensive outfits are nothing more than evidence of how sin has impacted the world. They are just elaborate cloth reminders of the first fig leaves.

That's one of the reasons why sex is such a powerful experience. It allows us to remove our clothes—symbolically removing the evidence of our failure. The intention within marriage is to once again be naked and feel no shame. A piece of the Garden of Eden is restored through rightly expressing a holy and honorable love.

Here's what we must understand: We'll only find that kind of fulfillment when we experience sex within the context of a godly marriage. Only within the boundaries of a loving, committed, lifelong relationship can we let go of our fig leaves, let go of our shame, and let go of our anxieties. The foundation of commitment brings safety and alleviates shame, replacing it with honor. A marriage that honors God will bring intimacy that honors Him.

Why? Because embracing holiness and honor results in God's glory and our pleasure. The shame-based questions—*What if I get pregnant? What if I get a disease? What if he doesn't call me tomorrow? What if she doesn't want to be with me anymore?*—are tossed as unneeded and unwanted fig leaves. The only way we'll experience a sexual relationship that goes beyond the physical and allows us to become truly, intimately connected is through applying the design God has given us.

Sex is holy. Sex is meant to be honored and highly valued. When those conditions are met, we'll experience the intimacy and passion God intended within His timing and design.

How can you more clearly see sex as honorable and highly valuable in a world filled with the opposite message?

TWO BRIDGES

It has been said men are from Mars and women are from Venus. Cute expression, but the comparison quickly breaks down. The planets are too similar to compare to the vast differences in how men and women think, respond, and act. Some days, even in a great marriage, it feels more like we're comparing men and women to the sun and moon.

At the same time, we can all agree that men and women have equal value in God's eyes. This is made clear at the very beginning of Scripture when God declares that men

 For more on gender differences and achieving fulfillment in your marriage, read *Men Are Like Waffles, Women Are Life Spaghetti* by Bill and Pam Farrel (Harvest House, 2007).

and women were both created in His image (Genesis 1:27). I like how Matthew Henry explained that passage in his *Commentary on the Whole Bible:*

> "The woman was made of a rib out of the side of Adam; not made out of his head to rule over him, nor out of his feet to be trampled upon by him, but out of his side to be equal with him, under his arm to be protected, and near his heart to be beloved."[3]

Men and women are equally valuable but terrifically different. We're different when it comes to anatomy, emotions, language, and so forth—not better or worse in any of those areas, but different. And these differences should be celebrated, not just endured. What's more, none of those variances came about through an accident or mistake. God intentionally designed men and women in different ways, and He said that it was good. We dare not overlook or trivialize these diversities. They have a lot of application to the birds and the bees. In fact, God has "encoded" men and women to respond uniquely when it comes to sex and sexuality. You could say God has "rigged" this whole thing to require completion in Him.

Let's explore these differences by using an example of bridges men and women need to cross in order to experience sexual fulfillment. The two bridges are a physical bridge and an emotional bridge. Both are possessed by each gender, but they are reversed in the order that they must be crossed in order to find fulfillment.[4]

In general, women must first cross an emotional bridge and then a physical bridge in order to be fulfilled sexually. They need to feel honored and cherished, trusting in the faithfulness and dedication of their spouse. When those needs have been met and the emotional bridge has been crossed, then they're comfortable to become physical.

The reverse is often true of men. They first cross a physical bridge in order to experience sexual fulfillment. They are more visual, more tactile. They want to see and feel. When that bridge has been crossed, men are ready to cross the emotional bridge. I'm not saying physical intimacy isn't desirable or pleasing to women; I'm saying it generally must first be based in emotional security. And I'm not saying that men are animalistic and unemotional in their desires. The point is that each gender crosses the bridges in a different order.

To illustrate, think of the differences between sexually-driven books targeted toward women and sexually-charged material designed for men. (I'm not recommending or approving these books, of course—just illustrating.) Books written for women usually contain pages and pages of words telling a love story with the only picture on

---

 According to *Psychology Today,* male brains are characterized by "the drive to analyze, explore, and construct a system." Female brains have "empathizing tendencies, the drive to identify another person's emotions and thoughts, and to respond to them with an appropriate emotion."[5]

the front cover. Usually it's a bare and barrel-chested man tenderly holding a damsel in distress. The only picture is still aimed at the emotion of romantically being swept away.

Men's magazines, on the other hand, are filled with numerous pictures that may have an article or two thrown in somewhere. Even then, the articles are often pointless and sexually-charged. (Pornography includes both impure pictures *and* inflamed paragraphs or dialogue.) The differences between the two reveal the different bridges that men and women gravitate toward.

God's intent is to make "two become one." Both physical and emotional needs and desires are incorporated in sexual intimacy, so God wired sex to be expressed by a man and a woman coming together in wedlock. By helping each other cross their primary bridge, sex becomes giving instead of just receiving. It's honorable because it honors the other person and the distinct differences between the couple. The danger, however, is that both of the bridges can be exploited. For example, you may have heard the phrase, "Men use love to get sex, and women use sex to get love." The manipulation of the preferred bridge is selfish. This is a growing problem that causes real and lasting damage, which we'll discuss in Session 3 of this study.

Does the concept of these two bridges ring true for you? Why or why not?

In what ways have you seen those bridges exploited in today's culture?

How can those bridges be cherished instead of exploited?

Here's something I've found to be true: The people who experience the greatest sexual intimacy and excitement in today's world are those who've walked with God and with their spouse for years. That combination of faithfulness to the Lord and faithfulness to a spouse produces a greater passion than any other lifestyle can match. Such people have submitted their lives to the Lord in a way that they are seeking to honor, not just be pleased by, their spouse.

You won't see that in any beer commercials, though. Our culture tries to tell us that fulfillment comes from a wild lifestyle and a "little black book" filled with potential partners—and that those of us who choose to love God and remain faithful to one spouse are prudes. We're boring.

That's a lie, but it's endlessly reinforced because so many people have a misunderstanding about the source of our sexual desires.

Here's a challenge: See if you can list three examples of couples whose marriages exhibit faithful love. (They could be characters from movies and books, or they could be real-life examples.)

1.

2.

3.

GOD'S PLAN FOR SINGLENESS

God's plan for sex and sexuality includes those who are called by Him to live a life of singleness. Whether you're right where you thought you'd be in life or you're longing for more, God has a plan for you (see Proverbs 16:9).

1. **Singleness is not second best.** As Paul explained in 1 Corinthians 7, marriage is not for everyone. Our focus shouldn't be on marriage or singleness, but on fulfilling God's purpose for us—individually and collectively.

2. **A desire doesn't constitute a right.** Wanting to inherit lots of money, yearning for children, or aspiring to be famous doesn't mean we're entitled to any of those things. The same is true of those who long for a spouse. God wants us to find contentment wherever we are: "I am not saying this because I am in need, for I have learned to be content whatever the circumstances" (Philippians 4:11).

3. **Singleness means a sacrifice.** Just as Christ gave up His life for us, we're called to give our lives to Him. Whether married or single, God should take first place in our lives. While it's not that having a spouse would pull us away from God, more people around means more things to do. For singles, alone time with Jesus is simply at more of a premium. Take the opportunity to focus on Him and how He wants to use you for His glory.

 Listen to John Piper's sermon "Sex and the Single Person" and Carolyn McCulley's talk "We're Not on Hold: Biblical Femininity for Single Women" at *desiringgod.org*.

What characteristics do the couples you thought of display?

THE SOURCE OF SEXUAL DESIRE

I'll make it clear right off the bat: God is the source of sexual desire. These feelings and urges we have—they come from God. They're actually a gift from God. He gave us these desires for our enjoyment according to His plan. They may seem untimely, but they are God-given.

Unfortunately, Christians haven't always done a good job of communicating this truth within the church and out to the world. In fact, sometimes we've made it seem like the opposite is true: that sexual desires are evil and come from our flesh. Sometimes we shout "Don't, don't, don't" so often that people begin to hear, "Don't ever." People begin to hear that all desire is bad and should never be fulfilled.

What we should be communicating is not the incorrect desires but incorrect timing. "Wait." Wait for God's plan. Fall in love with Jesus first and then watch how He brings about the fulfillment of the desires He created you to carry.

Sexual desire comes from God, and He's intentionally given it to all of us. If you don't have any sexual desire, then something's wrong. We all have a sex drive at varying levels. God has given it to us for the furtherance of the human race *and* for enjoyment within the context of marriage.

Have you ever thought about why sex is enjoyable? God didn't have to make it that way. He could've created sex as an unpleasant experience—something we endure every once in a while in order to have children. Instead, God gave us sex and sexual desires as gifts of blessing. But He's asked us to be stewards of those gifts—to hold them and cherish them and protect them until marriage. And if we have that "I do" moment and step over the line, then those gifts can be released and enjoyed to their fullest extent.

Song of Songs is a helpful passage of Scripture revealing this reality clearly. Just look at how the book gets started:

> **"Let him kiss me with the kisses of his mouth—for your love is more delightful than wine. Pleasing is the fragrance of your perfumes; your name is like perfume poured out. No wonder the maidens love you! Take me away with you—let us hurry! Let the king bring me into his chambers"** (Song of Songs 1:2-4).

 Seventeen percent of young Christians said they "have made [sexual] mistakes and feel judged in church because of them" (*barna.org*).

And things only get more exciting from that point on!

In your view, why did God intend for sex to be enjoyable?

How does the enjoyable nature of sex increase the importance of seeing it as a gift given—to be unwrapped at the appropriate time?

For those of you who are single, your desires and singleness probably seem in contradiction. It's an issue of timing and sacrifice. Continue to trust the Lord and understand that a part of the Christian life is sacrifice. Sacrificing our will and even the fulfillment of our desires brings forth spiritual growth. Living joyfully within God's will is better than sex; it's far more fulfilling to wait and trust Jesus for your joy than to be sexually active outside of God's will.

God has a plan for sex and sexuality. It's a plan all of us can understand, and it's a plan all of us can follow. Yes, *all* of us—married or single, active or waiting. No matter what you've been told by today's culture, no matter what you've done or had done to you in the past, God's plan is the best way for you to live now and in the future.

APPLY TO LIFE

> **PRAY:** During your quiet times this week, talk with God about your desires, hopes, dreams, fears, and weaknesses when it comes to sex and sexuality. Ask God to conform your heart to His plan.

> **OBSERVE:** As you go about your week, keep an eye open for the different messages our culture communicates about sex and sexuality. These messages could come from movies, TV shows, advertisements, textbooks, people you speak with, and more. Carry a notebook, smartphone, or some other device you can use to jot down these observations as you see them. At the end of the week, ask yourself these questions:

1. What are the primary messages communicated by our culture?
2. What are the primary sources of those messages?
3. How do those messages compare with God's plan?

> **STUDY:** Continue memorizing 1 Thessalonians 4:1-6 by focusing on verses 3-5: "It is God's will that you should be sanctified: that you should avoid sexual immorality; that each of you should learn to control his own body in a way that is holy and honorable, not in passionate lust like the heathen, who do not know God."

cking

—Hive:

ust 3

As a native Houstonian, I know our city well. I know the best Tex-Mex restaurants. I know the best back roads to use when I need to avoid traffic. But to most people, Houston is known for space exploration (since NASA's Johnson Space Center resides just to our south). "Houston, we have a problem," is the famous quote from the Apollo 13 lunar mission that sealed our fame. That's how we earned the name "Space City."

Several cities in the United States are famous for a specific theme or culture. New York is the "City that Never Sleeps," and Philadelphia is the "City of Brotherly Love." Chicago is known as both the "Windy City" and the "City of Broad Shoulders." Unfortunately, other cities are famous for less wholesome reasons. For example, here are the Top 5 Most Promiscuous Cities in America, according to a recent study:

5. San Francisco, Calif.

4. Miami, Fla.

3. Pittsburgh, Pa.

2. Seattle, Wash.

1. Portland, Oreg.[1]

If someone were to research the Top 5 Most Promiscuous Cities in the Ancient World, Thessalonica would likely make the list. It was known for wickedness and immorality. That's one reason why a church plant was necessary and a primary reason why we're studying 1 Thessalonians 4. Dark places need bright lights, and sinful societies need solid churches.

THE MEAN STREETS OF THESSALONICA

In the apostle Paul's day, the city of Thessalonica was a happening metropolis. Positioned as a major stop on the *Via Egnatia*, an ancient trade route connecting Byzantium with Italy and Rome, Thessalonica was also a major port city—meaning it received high traffic by land and by sea. The hustle and bustle was brisk and crowded. Thessalonica's business brawn resulted in an active slave market, which meant merchants and business owners had access to cheap labor, freeing up the owners for mischief. The combination of location and cheap labor enabled Thessalonica to become one of the largest and most prosperous cities in the Roman Empire.

In addition, the people of Thessalonica enjoyed a great deal of freedom. The city was under Roman authority, but it became a "free city" in 42 B.C., which meant the leaders were given the privilege of writing some of their own laws, producing their own money, and more. They escaped much of the oppression other cities experienced at the hands of the Romans.

 Watch the *Birds and Bees* video for Session 3, available at *threadsmedia.com/birdsandbees*.

 Under Roman law, *paterfamilias* or "the head of the household" had absolute power. Fathers could sell their children just as they could any other property.

So the Thessalonians had lots of freedom, lots of leisure time, and lots of expendable money. All good things, but the combination can bring problems. Sounds similar to many Americans today. You don't have to look too far in history to see that when these factors come together, morality and virtue are tempted to take a hike.

What evidence from Western culture suggests we also have an abundance of freedom, time, and money?

How have you been affected personally by freedom, time, and money—both positively and negatively?

These factors resulted in two major elements of the Thessalonian culture that produced rampant promiscuity and other forms of sexual immorality. The first was prostitution. To put it plainly, prostitution was part of everyday life for many Thessalonians. They went to the market to get food, to the theater for entertainment, and to prostitutes to fulfill their sexual desires. Prostitution was an accepted part of society. In fact, prostitution was part of *religious* life for the Thessalonians. The Greco-Roman culture included people known as temple prostitutes. In the ancient world, these men and women were seen as representatives of specific deities, and engaging them sexually was viewed as a way of connecting with those deities. (Obviously, this wasn't a part of Judaism or Christianity, but pagan religions.)

So, in Thessalonian society, you would visit a temple, identify a temple prostitute, and have sex as a way of worshiping or communing with a god. It's shocking how humans can spin even religion to fulfill fleshly desires. Paul wrote about the destructiveness of this practice in a letter he sent to the church at Corinth, which was a city in the same region as Thessalonica:

> **"Do you not know that your bodies are members of Christ himself? Shall I then take the members of Christ and unite them with a prostitute? Never! Do you not know that he who unites himself with a prostitute is one with her in body? For it is said, 'The two will become one flesh.' But he who unites himself with the Lord is one with him in spirit. Flee from sexual immorality. All other sins a man commits are outside his body, but he who sins sexually sins against his own body" (1 Corinthians 6:15-18).**

What's your response to "he who sins sexually sins against his own body"?

 Polygamous relationships in the Bible weren't condoned, nor were they successful. David committed adultery despite having multiple wives. Jacob's wives, Rachel and Leah, were rivals, and Sarah was jealous of Hagar.

How do the consequences of sexual sins differ from non-sexual sins?

The second element of Thessalonian culture that led to sexual immorality was a poor view of marriage. Greco-Roman society didn't emphasize monogamy—making a commitment to develop physical and emotional intimacy with only one person. As a result, people ceased to view marriage as the holy and honorable institution God created it to be.

This cheapened view of marriage created a social system where people—especially men— were encouraged to engage in sexual relationships with multiple partners. In fact, the culture even developed separate social classes for different levels of sexual relationships. Look at what Demosthenes, a Greek statesman and speaker, said in one of his orations:

> "Mistresses we keep for the sake of pleasure, concubines for the daily care of our persons, but wives to bear us legitimate children and to be faithful guardians of our households."[2]

How would you describe our culture's view of marriage?

The poor view of marriage in the Roman Empire also made adultery commonplace. Here's how Seneca, a Roman philosopher, described the social scene of the time. He used the word *paramour*, which means a lover—especially an adulterous one:

> "Is there any woman that blushes at divorce now that certain illustrious and noble ladies reckon their years, not by the number of consuls, but by the number of their husbands, and leave home in order to marry, and marry in order to be divorced? . . . Is there any shame at all for adultery now that matters have come to such a pass that no woman has any use for a husband except to inflame her paramour? Chastity is simply a proof of ugliness."[3]

Take a moment to skim the descriptions of Thessalonian culture above. Underline the elements of their culture that are similar to our culture today.

What are some differences between society in ancient Thessalonica and today?

 In 2001, Fox Television launched a reality show called "Temptation Island." In this "game," singles tried to break up couples heading toward marriage. Fox execs thought it would be entertaining to watch how couples were affected by efforts to weaken and destroy commitment and fidelity.[4]

Temple prostitutes, rampant divorce, and immorality everywhere you looked—that was Thessalonica. That was the culture into which Paul brought the message of purity—of God's good and perfect design for sex and sexuality.

Purity wasn't an easy concept for those early believers who heard Paul's teaching and believed the message of the gospel. Many of them were Gentiles (non-Jews), which meant they'd grown up without hearing about God's plan for the world, for His children, and for intimacy. In order to live out Paul's coaching on purity, the Thessalonian believers had to reject everything they'd been taught about sex and sexuality; they had to reject the values of the world around them.

Through Paul, God was calling His followers to a new, radical vision in the midst of a sexually saturated society. And the same is true of us today. The Christian message about sex may appear dated and puritanical to some, but the reality is God's truth spans all generations, cultures, and fads. His directions are always applicable and always relevant.

A LOOK AT LUST

Even when we agree with God's plans, we can still struggle with our desires. So before we go any further, we need to consider the issue of lust. If sexual desire comes from God—if it was designed to be positive—how does it turn into something negative like lust or sexual immorality? That's a good question, and fortunately it has a clear answer.

Before reading any further, write down your own definition of lust.

How have people's opinions of lust changed throughout the years, both individually and as a society?

Here's a simple definition for our study: *Lust is sexual desire that requires sin in order to be fulfilled.* It's the moment when you feel an urge or a desire, but in order to satisfy that desire you must turn your back on God's plan. Lust requires sin, just as all sexual immorality requires sin.

Sexual desire is a pure gift from God, but what makes our desires impure is our self-centered commitment to follow those desires in a way that's contrary to God's will and at the expense or exploitation of others. In other words, any urge is evil or lustful when we desire it so much that we're willing to sin in order to get it.

....

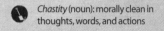 *Chastity* (noun): morally clean in thoughts, words, and actions

It's a glance that turns into a fantasy, for example—an urge that turns into an action or a thought that needs to be relished more in order to satisfy. The "on ramp" may be somewhat innocent, but the end of the road is sin. An ancient Chinese proverb sums it up well: You can't stop a bird from flying in front of your face, but you can stop it from making a nest on your head.

How do you react to the definition of lust as a sexual desire that requires sin in order to be fulfilled? Why?

Combating lust was Paul's aim in writing 1 Thessalonians 4:3-7:

> **"It is God's will that you should be sanctified: that you should avoid sexual immorality; that each of you should learn to control his own body in a way that is holy and honorable,** *not in passionate lust like the heathen, who do not know God; and that in this matter no one should wrong his brother or take advantage of him. The Lord will punish men for all such sins, as we have already told you and warned you.* **For God did not call us to be impure, but to live a holy life"** (emphasis added).

Re-write the italicized portion of these verses in your own words.

I want to highlight some things from these verses. First, lust isn't a solitary sin. It always leads us to "wrong" or to "take advantage" of others (v. 6). This is obvious when sexual immorality includes another person. When two people engage in sexual activity outside of God's will, they wrong each other. They drag each other deeper and deeper into sin and disobedience; they pull each other farther away from God's plan for purity. Ironically, they actually distance themselves from each other, too. What unifies them physically for a time creates disunity in their relationship—either quickly or over time—because of the feelings that develop, such as uncertainty, jealousy, self-defeat, doubt, worry, and anger.

Even if our lust is solitary—if it only involves our private thoughts or private actions—we still involve other people. When a man fantasizes lustfully about a woman, he wrongs her. When a woman dresses provocatively in order to gain attention from the men around her, she takes advantage of those men. Each causes damage and becomes a stumbling block for themselves and the other people involved.

 "I made a covenant with my eyes
not to look lustfully at a girl ...
Does he not see my ways and
count my every step?" (Job 31:1,4).

Again, because of how pervasive sexual immorality has become in our culture, we're often tempted to make a separation between thoughts and actions. We feel like lust or fantasy in our minds is *way* different from actually having a physical relationship with another person. After all, if we're only thinking about doing something, we're not actually *doing* anything. What's the problem with a few stolen glances or a revealing outfit? Right?

That's not how Jesus saw it, though:

> **"You have heard that it was said, 'Do not commit adultery.' But I tell you that anyone who looks at a woman lustfully has already committed adultery with her in his heart" (Matthew 5:27-28).**

Lust is sin. And God punishes sin. It doesn't matter if that sin involves only thoughts in our minds. It doesn't matter if we grew up in a culture that celebrates lust and we have to change our entire way of thinking in order to obey God—that's what the Thessalonians had to do. And it's the same for us.

Sin is never really solitary. It affects and infects the entire community. Think of how the lust of our culture affects society as a whole. Relationships are dragged down as lust is built up.

Second, consider the consequences of lust. In the second part of 1 Thessalonians 4:6, Paul stated,

> **"The Lord will punish men for all such sins, as we have already told you and warned you."**

Since lust is sin, it has eternal consequences. Wronging others in this way is wronging God. Thankfully, Christ has taken our punishment by His death. This is the good news that lustful hearts can be made new in Him. Unbelievers are called to place their faith in Christ as Savior, and believers are called to walk in the power that comes from a relationship with Him.

How do you react to reading that God punishes people for lust and "all such sins" (1 Thessalonians 4:6)?

Do you agree that lust always wrongs and takes advantage of other people? Why or why not?

 For an in-depth discussion of lust, check out Jared C. Wilson's Bible study *Seven Daily Sins: How the Gospel Redeems Our Deepest Desires* (available at *threadsmedia.com*).

How is Christ our only hope in regard to lust?

As I've mentioned, men and woman are aroused and tempted differently. A woman's lust is often romantic, while a man's lust is generally visual. My friend Beverly Parrish has ministered to women for years as a Baptist Collegiate Ministry associate director on several college campuses. Consider her thoughts on this subject:

> "There are seemingly harmless things women read, watch, and discuss that feed a lust for romance (chick flicks, "The Bachelor," *Twilight* books, etc.). For women, these things don't seem as 'sexual' or 'dirty' as pornography or graphic sexual content, so they think there is no sin in it. However, just like pornography, unrealistic expectations and fantasies are created. Young women then find that they cannot be satisfied by the romance they receive from a 'normal guy' (and the poor guys never feel like they measure up). Women need to guard what they watch and read."

Romantic movies and novels sear our minds with fantasy and make reality a disappointment. Whether it's the model's airbrushed body or the perfectly crafted romantic words of a novel or movie, both can lead us on the wrong path.

What are your thoughts on the differences between romantic and visual lust? What differences have you seen between men and women in this area?

How can the differences between men and women actually be a blessing to marriage when these desires combine to honor God?

All of us have felt the burn of lust in our hearts. I have. You have. Men have. Women have. Every adult walking around on this planet today has experienced lust. And the more we feed our lusts, the hungrier they get.

The good news is, through Jesus Christ, our pasts can be made pure and our futures have great possibilities. (We'll explore that reality more deeply in Session 5.) In order to make that happen, however, we'll need to do a little work. We'll need to gain a better understanding of the culture in which we live, and we'll need to explore some of the snares and temptations that can knock us away from God's pure plan for sex and sexuality.

....

 "Lust is the ape that gibbers in our loins.... Just when we think we're safe from him, he raises up his ugly head and smirks, and there's no river in the world flows cold and strong enough to strike him down." —Frederick Buechner, *Godric: A Novel*[5]

SESSION THREE BIRDS AND BEES

TWO MORE WORDS

In Session 2, we looked at two words that summarize God's plan for the birds and the bees. He created sex to be *holy* and *honorable*. Our culture views sex differently. In fact, our culture has inverted God's plan and values for sex and sexuality. We can get a clear sense of this by exploring two more words.

The first word is *excess*. Sex is everywhere in our culture. It affects everything. God created sex to be holy—to be set apart and special—but society has made it commonplace and pervasive. Sexual innuendo has saturated our society like water in a sponge.

You don't need to look any further than your TV to see what I'm talking about. According to a recent study, 75 percent of all prime-time programs contain sexual content. Contemplate that for a moment: Three out of every four shows being aired during prime time are sexually charged. The same report found that women in TV commercials are as likely to be shown in suggestive clothing, partially clad, or nude as they are to be fully clothed. In other words, every other woman you see in a commercial will be involved in something sexually suggestive.[6]

From the time you started watching TV until now, what changes have you seen in the content of TV programs?

How have you altered your viewing habits as a result of those changes?

The second word is *access*. We have access to more avenues for lust and sexual immorality than any other people in the history of the world. To make matters worse, the access can be private and secretive. That's just the unfortunate reality we have to deal with.

THREE TIPS FOR BATTLING LUST

1. **Watch what you watch.** What's going into your eyes (and your ears) is traveling to your heart.

2. **Let lust lead to prayer instead of sin.** When you have a lustful thought, begin to pray for that person. It is impossible to pray and lust at the same time.

3. **Fill your mind with the Bible and your friendships with character.** Reading God's Word and walking through life with godly people is crucial to winning the battle.

 Read the remainder of Jesus' Sermon on the Mount in Matthew 5–7. It represents Jesus' expectations for those who have followed Him as disciples, both ancient and modern.

Of course, a lot of that has to do with the Internet. Most experts say no matter where you start online, you're never more than three clicks away from pornographic material. But it's not just the Internet. It's movies on smartphones in our pockets. It's magazines at the gas station. It's video games now being produced with sex scenes.

We have access to lust-inducing material all day, every day. We're hit with an excess of sexual immorality seemingly everywhere we look. And that's one of the main reasons we have so much trouble following God's pure plan for sex and sexuality.

Here's what we need to understand if we're going to survive in today's culture: Living pure lives begins with controlling our eyes and our minds.[7] This is especially true for men—remember the first bridge they typically cross is physical, which incorporates the visual.

> **"The eye is the lamp of the body. If your eyes are good, your whole body will be full of light. But if your eyes are bad, your whole body will be full of darkness. If then the light within you is darkness, how great is that darkness!" (Matthew 6:22-23).**

What you allow yourself to view and what you allow yourself to think about will go a long way toward determining whether you remain faithful to God and faithful to your current or possible future spouse—both mentally and physically.

Do you agree that purity begins in the eyes and the mind? Why or why not?

In what ways does our culture seek to influence us through our eyes? Our minds?

What steps can you take to guard your eyes and your mind against these influences?

PORNOGRAPHY

Let's talk about one specific example of excess and access that's so dangerous in today's world. Please hear my heart when I say this: As a society, we're dying from Internet pornography. We're surrounded by it, and we're drowning in it.

 "Most women are not interested in pornographic images; they tend to prefer chat rooms, where they can connect with a person . . . Men have the opposite pattern—they prefer porn or adult sites, using chat rooms as their second choice for engaging in sexual activities." —Robert Weiss, *Untangling the Web*[8]

I don't want to throw too many statistics at you, but the following will help you get an idea of pornography's staggering impact in the world today:

- The largest pornographic Web site processes more than 4.4 billion page views each month, which makes it three times the size of *CNN.com* and *ESPN.com*.

- Up to 30 percent of the data transferred across the Internet is pornographic.[9]

- The porn industry earns between $10 to $14 billion every year. (That's more money than the *combined* revenues of the National Football League, National Basketball Association, and Major League Baseball.)

- More than 25 percent of search engine requests are for pornography (68 million every day).[10]

- More than 70 percent of men aged 17-34 will visit a pornographic site in a given month.[11]

Don't let the last stat fool you, because pornography has never been just for men. In fact, one out of every six women struggles with an addiction to pornography. And 90 percent of children between the ages of 8 and 16 have experience with Internet porn.[12]

How do you react to these statistics?

We need to understand what pornography really is: It's peppermint poison. It tastes sweet for a moment, and it may briefly satisfy your longings and desires when it comes to sex. But it's more than dangerous. It's a deadly poison, and it produces an unquenchable appetite for more.

I remember the first time I came face-to-face with online pornography. I was searching for something on my computer, and after a simple misspelling, images of girls started appearing on the screen. Thankfully, my wife, Kelly, was sitting next to me, and I just turned the computer toward her and said: "I don't know what I clicked on, but I need you to fix it. I'm out." Neither of us felt a surge of lust; we felt anger. How could it be so easy to end up on such a Web site? That's why pornography is so insidious. The ease of access and the hook of temptation can leverage a typing mistake into the beginning of a path leading to pain, confusion, and entrapment.

 If you need more information on overcoming a struggle with pornography go to *newlife.com*. Or if you'd like to talk with someone, call 800-NEW-LIFE (639-5433).

Here's another insidious thing about porn: Even images seen only for a split second can smolder in your mind for years.

That was the first time I experienced Internet pornography, and by God's strength it was also the last. I don't say that out of pride, but to offer an encouragement that God has called us to victory, and we *can* be victorious. *You* can be victorious over pornography.

Remember, the battle for purity is won in the eyes and the mind. If you've been involved with pornography, or if you're involved with it now, I plead with you to stop. I plead with you. Talk to someone who can offer help and accountability, because it's killing you even as it feels like it's pleasing you. It's destroying you click by click, but you can stop.

Peter Kreeft wisely states how pornography lessens our view of sex:

> "Sexual pornography means seeing the human body merely as an object of sexual desire and gratification, not as an instrument of self, the subject, the soul. Such 'soul categories' as promise, choice, commitment, and even love are suppressed or trivialized. But this is the deepest meaning of sexuality— it is something we *are* in our souls, our inner beings, not just something we *do* with our bodies."[13]

In order to help neutralize the temptation the Internet brings, all of the computers at Houston's First Baptist Church, where I pastor, have protection. We have filters and accountability. We utilize *x3watch.com,* which sends each staff member's Internet history to two people to ensure accountability. My Web history is sent monthly to my cousin and our executive pastor, for example.

If you've never indulged in pornography, be thankful. If you don't struggle with it now, don't look down your nose at the people in your life who do. Help them instead of judging them. Offer them forgiveness and love and compassion. They need you to help with the rescue.

What consequences have you seen in our culture from pornography's addictive power?

If you're struggling with pornography, to whom can you turn for help? What's preventing you from doing so?

GETTING PHYSICAL

Purity begins in the eyes and the mind, and the world attacks us with access to an excess of temptations in both of those areas. But the battle for purity doesn't end with the mind. What starts with the eyes and the mind can quickly move to the body.

If you're married, use your eyes and your mind to desire your spouse. And you should rejoice when that enjoyment moves naturally toward sexual expression. (This is something we'll discuss more in Session 6.) When you're married, you have to protect your union with your spouse. But what about when you're single? Let's spend a few moments exploring how God's plan for sex applies to physical intimacy outside the context of marriage.

How Far Is Too Far?

This is the million dollar question. When two people are dating, they spend a lot of time together. The more time they spend together, the more affection they feel for each other. And the more affection they feel for each other, the more they want to express that affection—verbally, emotionally, and physically. And so the question always surfaces: How far can we go physically before we start to sin?

How have you been taught to answer that question? How would you answer it today?

How does the church answer that question? How does our culture answer it?

Asking, "How far is too far?" is the wrong way to approach the issue because it almost always leads us down a compromising path into sin. I like what Halim Suh wrote about this topic in the book *Creation Restored*:

> "We experience this all the time. We want to know where the line is between 'right' and 'wrong' so we can get as close to it as possible without going over. We think we can enjoy ourselves more if we're closer to that line, and we're confident we'll never cross it. But we always do.

> "As a pastor, I get those questions all the time: How far is too far? When is it officially sex? Pornography is OK if I'm not cheating on my wife, right? What am I allowed to do as a Christian?

> "It's foolishness. If we keep trying to hug the line, we're going to cross the line. And we know it."[15]

---

 to steward: the act of utilizing and managing all resources God provides for the glory of God and the betterment of creation[14]

Remember, the goal of sex is to glorify God. But when we try to figure out how much we can gratify our flesh, we're moving the focus away from God and back onto ourselves.

Paul wrote about this mind-set in Romans 8:

> "Those who live according to the sinful nature have their minds set on what that nature desires; but those who live in accordance with the Spirit have their minds set on what the Spirit desires. The mind of sinful man is death, but the mind controlled by the Spirit is life and peace; the sinful mind is hostile to God. It does not submit to God's law, nor can it do so. Those controlled by the sinful nature cannot please God" (vv. 5-8).

So the question should not be, *How close can I get to sin without actually sinning?* Rather, we should ask: *How can I glorify God through this relationship? How can we steward our gift of sexuality in a way that honors Jesus?*

According to the Scripture passage above, what are the symptoms of a mind "controlled by the sinful nature"? What about a mind "controlled by the Spirit"?

Why is it impossible to please God when we're "controlled by the sinful nature"?

If we're focused on stewarding the gift of our bodies, all of the questions about physical intimacy really boil down to one thing: to kiss or not to kiss. That is the question.

Think about it: When we're talking about a physical relationship, anything beyond kissing is foreplay. (Some may argue kissing is, too.) And the whole purpose of foreplay is to lead people into sex. And even kissing isn't a given. You need to decide if you can kiss and maintain a focus on pleasing God at the same time.

When Kelly and I were dating, a kiss was the line. Thankfully, we came to the wedding altar having only kissed. This was very important to both of us. Having made mistakes in previous relationships, I had set a goal before I even met Kelly. My desire was to be able to ask my future father-in-law for his daughter's hand and say, "I have never touched your daughter in an inappropriate way." Fighting to keep my eyes on the Lord and flee temptation, I was able to make that statement to Kelly's dad, and I'm grateful to this day.

I was nervous the day I asked Charles (Kelly's dad) to marry his youngest daughter. He's a typical Texas rancher with a truck, boots, a cowboy hat, and guns. (It wasn't the boots that made me nervous; it was the guns!) I asked if I could talk with him privately, and we walked out into the backyard. Fearful of eye contact and knowing what was coming, we both looked at the ground as I gave my speech—or tried to. Even though I'm a professional speaker all I could get out was, "I love her and I want to marry her." He responded with a question: "You got any money in the bank?" Truly, that was the question! Thankfully, I had been saving and answered with the affirmative.

As the conversation ended, I told him of the purity of our dating. He said he appreciated my respect for Kelly, him, and her mother, Julie, and then we walked back to the house. As I thought about our conversation, I sensed the pleasure of God. Though I had made mistakes in the past, this time I got it right. My future wife and I were headed to marriage unscathed by immorality.

Decide what the holy and godly line will be in your relationships. Disconnect from past guilt and commit to the future goal. If you stumble, get back up. Remember that physical intimacy is intended to bring glory to God within marriage. Forgo the short-term lustful desires for the long-term blessing.

Read Elisabeth Elliot's perspective, from her book, *Passion and Purity*:

> "The greater the potential for good, the greater the potential for evil. . . . A good and perfect gift, these natural desires. But so much the more necessary that they be restrained, controlled, corrected, even crucified, that they might be reborn in power and purity for God."[16]

Do you agree "the greater the potential for good, the greater the potential for evil"?

What boundaries have you set in place for physical intimacy before marriage?

 Listen to "Down" by Jason Walker and "Forgiveness" by Patty Griffin from the *Birds and Bees* playlist, available for purchase at *threadsmedia.com/birdsandbees*.

How do you respond to claims that it's not realistic for people to date without becoming physically intimate?

Casual Encounters

In addition to grappling with "how far is too far" within a dating relationship, many people are considering the implications of physical intimacy without any kind of relationship at all, also known as "casual sex."

One common approach to casual sex is "hooking up." Two people have some kind of spontaneous sexual encounter—usually at a party and usually after consuming a lot of alcohol. These encounters range from making out to oral sex and beyond.

The second approach is "friends with benefits" or "friends with privileges." Two people conclude they're just too busy or uninterested in forming a committed relationship, but they still have lustful desires and sexual urges. So they find a friend who'll give them sexual gratification without a relationship or responsibility. They falsely assume they can have sex without strings attached.

We desperately need to understand the consequences of these practices, both spiritually and practically.

Spiritually, both of these practices are symptoms of the way our culture has de-valued sex. They dishonor sex as God intended it to be experienced. They turn what was supposed to be honorable into something base and animalistic—just another itch that needs to be scratched. Practically, casual sex has never led people to feel fulfilled and joyful in their lives. It only leads to pain, frustration, and irreversible regrets.

In her book *Sex and the Soul*, Donna Freitas interviewed young adults about their sexual experiences and spiritual beliefs. When she asked them to describe how they felt the morning after a hook up, the most common answer was a mix of regret, shame, and disgust.

One student wrote:

> "Feel bad about myself . . . Disgusted with my decision (not consistent with what I believe). Feel empty. I wonder: Does the . . . guy really want more? Was it just sex and if it was, [was] I . . . just an object? . . . I degraded myself."

 In February 2012, U.S. News (on *msnbc.com*) reported that students at Yale University took a stand against the "sexual obsession" on their campus. They had simply seen enough of the hookup culture to know that it's not healthy, but rather deeply damaging—and they wanted their friends and peers to reconsider.

SESSION THREE BIRDS AND BEES

Another said:

> "Most of the time my stomach is in a knot and I try to suppress memories of the night before, misplaced guilt wells up, and I am somewhat miserable. But I think it's a good thing—I think that is life: the night of beauty, wonder, and arousal, the morning of destructive thought and regretful recollection."[17]

When I read something like that, I want to shout: *No! That's not how life is supposed to be. That's not what God created us to experience, and it's not how God planned for us to feel. His plan is so much better!* God's plan for sex involves beauty and wonder and arousal, yes. That's what He intended for us. But He gave us that gift within the context of a loving, committed marriage so that we never have to experience the misery of shame and regret, among many other destructive consequences.

TO THE HEART

Let's move from the birds and the bees and focus on our hearts. Discussions like this one can bring feelings of desire, discouragement, or despair. Guilt over past mistakes can creep up and lay over us like a blanket of shame.

Please don't stay there. Jesus is an able sacrifice for our sin—even sexual sin or lustful actions. He not only can but wants to bring healing and wholeness. Turn to Him in prayer and trust. Trust in the healing message of 1 Peter 2:24:

> **"He himself bore our sins in his body on the tree, so that we might die to sins and live for righteousness; by his wounds you have been healed."**

A conversation like this can also bring unusual feelings to those who have not "kicked the beehive" in dramatic ways. Sure, we've all had thoughts, but the actions have been minor compared to our culture. If that's the case for you, I want to encourage you that you haven't missed out on anything but pain. Sometimes we convince ourselves that the roller coaster ride of sin is a thrill, but that's not the case. The thrill is successfully and proudly walking with God in purity. Be thankful and continue to walk the right road. Additionally, make an effort to extend grace to those who have strayed from God's design for sex and sexuality. Many people are hurting, and they need encouragement to find and embrace God's plan for their lives. The best testimony is one of purity and waiting, seeking, and trusting God.

 Whether you're a college student waiting for school to end, a young professional waiting on your career to take off, or simply a young adult waiting on a big change to take place, *InTransit: What Do You Do With Your Wait?* by Mike Harder shows how waiting for God's calling deepens our understanding of His timing and faithfulness (*threadsmedia.com*).

APPLY TO LIFE

> **PRAY:** Work on letting what you've learned sink in this week by specifically praying about the following three things every day. You've been reading words on a page for three chapters now, so take the time for a major upgrade and talk directly with Jesus.

> 1. Confess past actions or thoughts to Him.
> 2. Declare your desire to live for His glory today.
> 3. Thank Him for His love and ask Him to be your fulfillment.

> **OBSERVE:** Spend some time this week researching the different types of accountability filters and software on the market. Identify which version would work best in connection with your use of the Internet—including tablets, smartphones, and other devices—and consider making a purchase. Here are three good places to start researching:

> 1. XXX Church (*x3watch.com*)
> 2. Safe Eyes (*internetsafety.com/safeeyes*)
> 3. Covenant Eyes (*covenanteyes.com*)

> **STUDY:** Continue memorizing 1 Thessalonians 4:1-8 by focusing on verse 6: "And that in this matter no one should wrong his brother or take advantage of him. The Lord will punish men for all such sins, as we have already told you and warned you."

During high school, one of my teachers assigned us a paper on the most interesting person we knew. So I chose to write my paper about my Uncle Bobby. He was one of my favorite people. Sharply dressed with a quick wit, you never knew exactly what Uncle Bobby would say, but it was usually funny.

Uncle Bobby drove a grayish blue Porsche 911, which only added to my reverence of him. After a family trip to Pensacola, Florida, Uncle Bobby tossed me the keys to drive back to his home in New Orleans. At 16 years old, I was behind the wheel of a Porsche 911 with only one instruction from its owner: "Don't go slow." My gleeful reply was simply, "Yes, sir." I loved my Uncle Bobby, and so did the rest of my family.

When I was 17, I vividly remember the day my mom sat me down to talk a few weeks before Christmas. "I need to tell you something," she said with an unusual seriousness. "Uncle Bobby is gay, and he has AIDS." My heart broke. I had been curious about his sexual orientation but the diagnosis of AIDS was an unexpected bomb. Weeks later I shared a prayer request for his healing with some friends, and I can still remember weeping as I tried to get the words out.

Christmas was the first time I saw Uncle Bobby after hearing the news. I remember my internal struggle: *What am I going to do when I see Uncle Bobby?* At that time, I didn't understand how AIDS spread, so I didn't know if I would have to keep my distance or if things would be normal, like before. Those hesitations fell away when I walked through the door and saw my uncle. I embraced him with a long hug. In my teenage mind and growing faith I thought, *If I get AIDS, I get AIDS—but I'm hugging my uncle.*

I tell you this story because I want you to understand my mind-set as we approach the issue of homosexuality. I'm not writing this as an angry preacher but a broken-hearted family member. I'm not writing this with a sense of vindictiveness or spite.

Rather, I'm writing this as one who has been a part of a family struggle. I watched Christians in my family ache through the balance of loving my uncle yet not approving of his choice to act out on his same-sex attraction. It's easy to swing one way or the other, but I've found it difficult to stand in the balance of "speaking the truth in love" (Ephesians 4:15). I'm approaching this topic as someone with compassion who wants to hug, not hit.

We can have an honest, grown-up, respectful, and loving conversation about homosexuality. I understand this will be difficult for many to discuss.

....

 "Instead, speaking the truth in love, we will in all things grow up into him who is the Head, that, Christ" (Ephesians 4:15).

How have you been personally affected by homosexuality?

What are your thoughts on homosexuality?

Would you say your mind is made up regarding homosexuality, or are you open to learning more?

The One who created humanity has designed us to operate sexually according to a plan that brings glory to Him and fulfillment for us. With that in mind, here's the big question we're going to explore in this session: Why does God's plan for sex and sexuality include only heterosexuality?

To answer this question, the rest of this session will focus on five categories often connected with homosexuality. Pretend you're comfortably seated in your living room with five coffee cups representing each category. Those five coffee cups represent personal history, human biology, today's society, personal desire, and the Bible. Let's get started.

COFFEE CUP 1: PERSONAL HISTORY

In my experience, whenever a conversation about homosexuality begins, the first questions that start flying usually surround orientation and personal choice. For example: How do people come into a homosexual lifestyle? Are people born gay? Are people predisposed to choose one lifestyle over another? Is there such a thing as a gay gene?

Those questions really boil down to one: Do people have a choice when it comes to their sexual orientation?

How would you answer that question? Why?

What answers to this question have you heard from today's culture?

 Watch the *Birds and Bees* video for Session 4, available at *threadsmedia.com/birdsandbees*.

What answers have you heard from churches and individual Christians?

Evidence supports both sides of the being "born gay" theory. Some studies and statistics suggest people have no choice about their orientation; other studies and statistics suggest people have all the choice in the world. Regardless of the DNA debates, three aspects of influence are common:

1. Parental Relationships. Boys being disconnected from their dads and girls from their moms can result in wondering and then fantasizing about what it means to be loved by the same gender. Furthermore, absent or emotionally-deficit parents cause issues from a lack of nurture, physical presence, and physical touch.

2. Sexual Abuse. The Archives of Sexual Behavior reports that "46 percent of homosexual men and 22 percent of homosexual women reported having been molested by a person of the same gender."[1] Child sex-abuse expert David Finkelhor found that "boys victimized by older men were over four times more likely to be currently engaged in homosexual activity than were non-victims."[2]

3. Early Sexualization. For example, early exposure to porn. Dr. Milton Magness, a former staff member of the Julianna Poor Counseling Center at our church, is a certified sex addiction therapist and a licensed professional counselor. He explained to me that we all have an arousal template, a shaping of our understanding of arousal and preparation for sex. Early exposure to sex distorts that template. The average first exposure to pornography today is 11 years old.[3] Additionally, researchers have found that "90 percent of children over the age of 11 have been exposed to Internet pornography."[4]

Another interesting study, conducted in 2010 in Sweden, interviewed a group of 7,600 identical twins in an effort to see how sexual orientation played out when two people were almost identical on a biological level. In other words, they wanted to see if people with the same genetic material developed the same sexual orientation. Of the 7,600 twins who participated, the study found 33 cases where both of the twins were gay. The study found 252 cases where one twin was homosexual while the other was heterosexual. And the rest of the cases—the vast majority—had both twins identify themselves as heterosexual.[5]

So you had a tiny minority of twins who both identified themselves as homosexual and a vast majority of twins who both identified themselves as heterosexual. And in the middle was a significant group where one twin differed from the other despite having the same

---

 More information and help from Milton Magness can be found at *hopeandfreedom.com*.

genetic makeup. This research on twins supports the conclusion that there's no scientific proof that people are born with a homosexual orientation or hereditary disposition.

Even if we concede the point and assume that people do have a genetic predisposition toward either homosexuality or heterosexuality—that someone is born gay or straight— the bottom line is this: A predisposition toward a certain behavior does not change the moral implications or consequences of that behavior. In other words, many people are born with a predisposition toward alcoholism or other addictions, but that doesn't mean they should be encouraged to act on those predispositions.

I easily raise my hand of admission, "I'm a lustful man, predisposed toward adultery." But it doesn't make adultery the right behavior, and I'm choosing to live faithfully to my wife.

How do you react to the idea that all people are born with a predisposition toward sin? What's the biblical support for that idea? (See Romans 5:12-21 and Ephesians 2:1-5.) Does it mean we're excused from the consequences?

What evidence of that predisposition have you seen in today's society? In your own life and behavior?

COFFEE CUP 2: HUMAN BIOLOGY
The second category I want to address is our biological makeup. Specifically, what do our bodies tell us about the practice of homosexuality?

Many people don't realize practicing homosexuals experience significantly higher rates of depression and suicide. For example, a recent study found that homosexual adults were at least 50 percent more likely than heterosexual adults to have a history of depression and anxiety disorders.[6] Even more startling, another study indicated that lesbian, gay, and bisexual teens are five times more likely to attempt suicide than their heterosexual peers.[7] Those are shocking numbers. So what is causing homosexuals to experience higher levels of suicide and depression?

One cause is cultural oppression. Homosexual men and women likely experience more depression and anxiety because they're looked down upon or bullied by heterosexuals. That's certainly a factor and, of course, abusing or mistreating people for any reason is contrary to the teachings of Jesus.

 Listen to "The Struggle" by Tenth Avenue North and "The Hurt & The Healer" by MercyMe from the *Birds and Bees* playlist, available for purchase at *threadsmedia.com/birdsandbees*.

What's your earliest memory of being mistreated because you were different?

What impact did that mistreatment have on you at the time? Did it have any long-term consequences?

Still, we need to determine whether cultural oppression is the main reason why homosexual men and women experience higher rates of suicide and depression. And there's plenty of evidence that other factors exist. Some of the most applicable evidence comes from a study conducted in the Netherlands, where gay marriage is legal and homosexuality is widely accepted. The study concluded that, even in a sympathetic culture, homosexual individuals are at a substantially higher risk for suicide, major depression, and anxiety disorders.[8]

Why do you think these statistics are this way?

How can depression open a ministry door to help homosexuals discover Christ?

One key factor behind these statistics is that our bodies simply weren't designed for homosexual interaction. Men especially were not designed to experience sexual intercourse with other men. Common sense recognizes that sexually, men and women were designed as a complementary fit.

Take it even further. If something is truly amoral—meaning it's without moral consequences, like choosing between Coke or Pepsi—then everyone should be able to participate in either option. In other words, if a homosexual lifestyle and a heterosexual lifestyle are equally part of God's design for humanity, then all of humanity should be able to choose either one. We can all eat, for example. We can all walk, talk, love, give, and receive without limit.

But that's not the case with homosexuality. Looking at it practically, if everyone adopted a homosexual lifestyle, the human race would end. The practice of homosexuality cannot produce life, which is a major part of God's plan for sex and sexuality. It's difficult

---

 James 3:9-10 makes it clear that all human beings are created in the image of God and are worthy of love and respect.

to believe in both evolution and homosexuality. Yet these two beliefs are held and espoused frequently together. A homosexual's inability to reproduce hinders the passing on of a "gay gene."

In fact, the opposite is true—instead of passing on life, homosexuality actually brings death. I say this with a heavy heart. In 2007, the Family Research Institute revealed research that the lifespan of a homosexual is on average 24 years shorter than that of a heterosexual.[9] It literally kills you:

> **"For the wages of sin is death, but the gift of God is eternal life in Christ Jesus our Lord" (Romans 6:23).**

Oh, my heart aches to ponder this.

As I arrived at the church in New Orleans for my Uncle Bobby's funeral, my eyes welled up with tears. He was deceased at 49 years old. After the priest finished his homily, as a first-time pallbearer, I grasped the coffin's handle along with the rest of the boutonniere-wearing men in suits. Some were gay friends and others straight family, but it didn't matter as we carried my uncle out of the church. I have two vivid memories: The first is seeing a black hearse with an open back door. The second is the shattered faces as the gay community of New Orleans attended yet another funeral.

I didn't know any statistics back then, but I knew in my heart that 49 years was too soon. My uncle's life ended too early, and it pains me deeply to think how many other lives are cut short. Biology declares our bodies were not made to practice homosexuality.

After pondering these sobering statistics of a shortened lifespan of those living in the homosexual lifestyle, write out a prayer for someone you know struggling with this.

COFFEE CUP 3: OUR SOCIETY

Modern society has a lot to say about homosexuality, especially when it comes to how many people identify themselves as gay or lesbian.

You may have heard, for example, that homosexuals make up more than 10 percent of the American population. That's actually not the case. The figure dates back to a sex researcher named Alfred Kinsey in 1948.[10] Fast-forward to the '70s when a man named Bruce Voeller publicized the statistic as a way of convincing the public and politicians that homosexuality was prevalent in the culture. Voeller was the chairman of the National

Gay Task Force, and he admitted several years later to misleading the public intentionally about the prevalence of homosexuality.[11] Voeller died in 1994 of an AIDS-related illness.

So what percentage of the population is actually gay?

In 2011, the National Center for Health Statistics and the Center for Disease Control and Prevention teamed up to answer that question, among others. The government-sponsored study found that only 1.4 percent of the population claimed a same-sex orientation. The number rose to 3.7 percent when bisexuals were included, as well.[12]

The same study also revealed that an overwhelming majority of people who identify themselves as homosexual don't practice homosexuality exclusively. In fact, 81 percent of homosexuals and bisexuals in the survey have experienced sex with at least one partner of the opposite gender—while only 6 percent of those claiming heterosexuality have experienced any kind of physical intimacy with a person of the same gender.[13]

A survey from the American Public Health Association reported that homosexual individuals had an average of 49 sexual partners during their lifetime, and between 8 and 12 percent of homosexuals had more than 500 partners during their lifetime.[14] Monogamy in the homosexual community is more rare than the heterosexual community. Among heterosexuals, "67.6 percent of men and 75.5 percent of women had only one sex partner in the previous year." Among homosexuals, "only 2.6 percent of men and 1.2 percent of women engaging in same-sex relationships" had restricted themselves to one partner.[15]

How do you react to those statistics?

Does the number of people who practice homosexuality influence your opinion about homosexuality as part of God's design? Why or why not?

Allow me to explain why those statistics matter. For decades, voices from within our society have claimed that homosexuality is a natural, unchangeable fact of life for tens of millions of Americans. Those voices have claimed that a homosexual lifestyle is an equal alternative to a heterosexual lifestyle—just like Coke is an equal alternative to Pepsi. Those voices have claimed that people have no more choice over their sexual orientation than they have over the color of their eyes.

Gary J. Gates, a demographer from the Williams Institute at the UCLA School of Law—a sexual orientation law and public policy think tank—estimated in 2011 that about 3.8 percent of Americans identified themselves as gay, lesbian, bisexual or transgender.[16]

These statistics reveal that there are a small number of people who identify themselves as homosexual—and a majority of those are conflicted about the decision. The struggle with homosexuality is real, but it is also not God-ordained. Many still feel a pull toward a heterosexual lifestyle, which makes sense because that's the lifestyle we were created to live. God created us to live according to a specific design for sex and sexuality, and we only cause damage to ourselves when we deviate from that design—whether we deviate in a way that's heterosexual or homosexual.

Armand Nicholai, chief psychiatrist of the Medical School at Harvard University and editor of the *Harvard Guide to Psychiatry,* has stated, "I have treated hundreds of homosexuals. None of them, deep down, thought it was normal. Simulating eating is not eating. Simulating being female is not being female. Simulating sex is not sex."[17]

What voices from our culture have you heard argue that homosexuality is a lifestyle without negative consequences?

The Gay Marriage Debate
When we're talking about the intersection of homosexuality and society, another issue repeatedly brought up is gay marriage. For centuries, marriage has been defined as the union of one man and one woman. That's how God designed things according to Genesis 2:

> **"But for Adam no suitable helper was found. So the LORD God caused the man to fall into a deep sleep; and while he was sleeping, he took one of the man's ribs and closed up the place with flesh. Then the LORD God made a woman from the rib he had taken out of the man, and he brought her to the man.**
>
> **"The man said, 'This is now bone of my bones and flesh of my flesh; she shall be called "woman," for she was taken out of man.'**
>
> **"For this reason a man will leave his father and mother and be united to his wife, and they will become one flesh" (vv. 20b-24).**

That first paragraph is important. Adam (representing all of mankind) was alone, and God created Eve (representing all of womankind) as a partner for him. Men and women were created for each other as a way to complement and complete the other. God intentionally designed two genders to join together and become "one flesh."

However, many people today—including many heterosexuals—believe that any two people in love should have the right to express that love within the context of marriage.

What opinions have you heard recently on the subject of gay marriage?

What's your own opinion on the topic?

Make a quick list of lifestyles that are amoral—meaning, they have no moral consequences. (Choosing to live in Houston instead of San Antonio, for example.)

How does a homosexual lifestyle compare and contrast to the list you made above?

I admit, it's hard to make an argument against gay marriage when you approach the issue from a civil rights perspective. If being gay is an amoral, unalienable right, then denying two consenting adults the opportunity to become married feels like trampling on their freedoms—and we love freedom.

But as I said earlier, these issues also need to be explored from a moral perspective. As Dennis Prager intriguingly points out, "There was not one major religious leader or thinker in Jewish or Christian history prior to the present generation who argued for same sex marriage."[18] Has something theologically new been discovered or have cultural opinions shifted?

The argument goes, "If two people are in love, why can't they get married?" But that leads to another question: Why limit marriage to two people? If we no longer use the definition of marriage as a union between one man and one woman, will we stop at just two men or two women? Can three consenting adults marry? Can it be husband, wife, and husband? Why not, if the definition of marriage is founded solely on desire and adult consent?

Here's what Charles Krauthammer wrote in *Time* magazine:

"For the time being, marriage is defined as the union 1) of two people 2) of the opposite sex. Gay-marriage advocates claim that restriction Number 2 is discriminatory, a product of mere habit or tradition or, worse, prejudice. But what about restriction Number 1? If it is blind tradition or rank prejudice to insist that those who marry be of the opposite sex, is it not blind tradition or rank prejudice to insist that those who marry be just two? In other words, if marriage is redefined to include two men in love, on what possible principled grounds can it be denied to three men in love?"[19]

What's your definition of marriage?

Another thing we need to consider as we explore the moral impact of marriage and society is the family. The family is the basic cell of any culture. It's the individual bricks that come together to make up the foundation of a society. Everything else—business, church, school, entertainment—is built on top of that foundation.

For this reason, families need to remain healthy and reproducible. That's another vital part of God's design, but it's not something that can be accomplished through gay marriage. Such families are not naturally reproducible.

The bottom line is this: If the cells of a civilization aren't healthy and reproducible, it won't be able to continue on. The civilization will crumble. And honestly, because of mankind's sin—both homosexual and heterosexual—we're beginning to see that already in today's society. We need to return to God's plan for marriage, sex, and sexuality.

COFFEE CUP 4: DESIRE
The next category I want to talk about is sexual desire, and it's especially tricky because it's especially personal. Many people think, *I feel a sexual desire for my gender, so why shouldn't I act on those desires?* On a general level, my response is to look back at 1 Thessalonians 4:7:

> **"For God did not call us to be impure, but to live a holy life."**

We're all sexual beings, and we all have sexual longings. Yet many of those desires—both heterosexual and homosexual—fall outside of God's plan for sexual fulfillment. Unchecked internal desires will birth external action.

Hear me loud and clear: Just because you have a homosexual thought (or even a series of thoughts) doesn't mean you are a homosexual. In today's culture, however, those "out of nowhere" thoughts are pinpointed and reinforced. The little spark is fanned into a flame because so many voices are commanding you to declare as early as possible whether you're gay or not gay. According to my friend and church member Richard Campbell, who lived a homosexual lifestyle for 25 years before being set free by Jesus, "To be 'gay' one has to not only embrace the lifestyle, but also believe that the lifestyle is healthy, moral, and 'right.' Men who struggle with homosexuality, who don't accept it, are not homosexuals. They are 'men who struggle with homosexuality.'" Unfortunately, these passing thoughts, if embraced, can lead to the next step of experimentation.

Experimentation generally begins when guys search for excitement without commitment and girls search for relationship without risk. Remember our bridges example from Session 2? Typically, when it comes to intimacy, men first cross the physical bridge and women first cross the emotional bridge. God has prepared sexual intimacy to be selfless— to require love and giving, not just the pursuit of personal fulfillment. For example, I've seen this happen often with women in college. A young woman develops a friendship that turns into codependence, ultimately producing jealousy and possessiveness; soon the swirl of emotions morphs into lesbian experimentation. It all begins with her desire for emotional connection, but our culture pushes her to advance those feelings and fan the flame of desire.

Why is experimentation never a good idea when it comes to desires?

For anyone tempted to experiment, I advise you to remain patient and refrain. Gain perspective by talking with people who've gone through the storms and can give you wise counsel. Trust me: A hormonal hurricane can be eventually calmed into sunny skies when you hang onto the anchor of Jesus.

"We have this hope as an anchor for the soul, firm and secure" (Hebrews 6:19).

When you're confused about something intellectually (think back to school, for example), where do you turn to find answers and gain clarity?

How could that process apply to confusion about sex and sexuality?

 Experimentation was clearly exemplified in Katy Perry's 2008 mainstream hit song, "I Kissed a Girl," aimed at teenage girls. The song spent seven weeks at number one on the charts and sold more than 2.5 million copies.

Who is a safe person you can turn to when wrestling through life's struggles?

COFFEE CUP 5: THE BIBLE

The big question we're addressing in this session is why God's plan for sex and sexuality includes only heterosexuality. We've worked to gain some insight on that question through the categories of personal history, human biology, today's society, and personal desires. Now let's look at what the Bible says.

Notice the Bible wasn't the starting place of our examination. Without including God in the conversation on homosexuality, we've already seen wounds in our personal history, failing physical bodies, a weakened society, and conflicting desires.

I'd like to point out that Christianity is not the only religion that expressly prohibits homosexual actions. Search any of the world's major belief systems, and you'll find that homosexuality is often considered both socially and morally wrong. For example, in Islam, the Koran states that homosexual actions are sinful and illegal; there's no degree of acceptance of the homosexual lifestyle. Judaism maintains that homosexuality is not God's design for sexuality, as supported in the Old Testament:

> **"For this reason a man will leave his father and mother and be united to his wife, and they will become one flesh" (Genesis 2:24).**

> **"Do not lie with a man as one lies with a woman; that is detestable" (Leviticus 18:22).**

Christianity incorporates these Old Testament beliefs and adds the truth that Jesus Christ saves us from our sin and guides us into a life that characterizes God's righteousness.

> **"Therefore God gave them over in the sinful desires of their hearts to sexual impurity for the degrading of their bodies with one another. They exchanged the truth of God for a lie, and worshiped and served created things rather than the Creator—who is forever praised. Amen. Because of this, God gave them over to shameful lusts. Even their women exchanged natural relations for unnatural ones. In the same way the men also abandoned natural relations with women and were inflamed with lust for one another. Men committed indecent acts with other men, and received in themselves the due penalty for their perversion" (Romans 1:24-27).**

 Until Jesus came as the fulfillment of the Old Testament Law, Leviticus 20 demanded the death penalty for those guilty of adultery, incest, fornication, and homosexuality.

"Do you not know that the wicked will not inherit the kingdom of God? Do not be deceived: Neither the sexually immoral nor idolaters nor adulterers nor male prostitutes nor homosexual offenders nor thieves nor the greedy nor drunkards nor slanderers nor swindlers will inherit the kingdom of God. *And that is what some of you were. But you were washed, you were sanctified, you were justified in the name of the Lord Jesus Christ and by the Spirit of our God*" (1 Corinthians 6:9-11, emphasis added).

What words or phrases from these verses catch your attention most? Why?

How does hearing other religious views affect your thoughts?

First Corinthians 6:9-11 is a great summary on the Bible's message concerning homosexuality, and I want to highlight four quick points from this passage:

1. The practice of homosexuality is not compatible with God's plan for sex and sexuality. It's a deviation from His plan, and it prevents us from experiencing the fulfillment God intends for us.

2. It's equally clear in the Bible that homosexuality is just one of many deviations from God's plan for sex and sexuality. It's no better or no worse than heterosexual deviations like lust, premarital sex, prostitution, or adultery. Often Christians have communicated homosexuality is a "unique" kind of sin, different than other "normal" sins. The biblical truth is that all sin is against God.

3. This Scripture affirms that homosexual desires are real. The apostle Paul makes it clear that people have struggled with homosexual desires since the beginning of the church—including people within the church.

4. It's also biblically clear that at least some people who struggle with homosexual desires can move past those desires and choose not to act on them—if they choose God's forgiveness and help. Paul says, "that is what some of you *were*" (v. 11). Healing comes through the saving power of Jesus Christ, His blood shed on our behalf, and the work of the Holy Spirit in our hearts. (We'll talk more about that in Session 5.)

How do you react to those four points? Why?

....

 Other biblical passages on homosexuality include Leviticus 20:13; Judges 19:22-30; and 1 Timothy 1:10.

What else does the Bible communicate about the topic of homosexuality?

Describe the hope found in the phrase "that is what some of you were" (v. 11).

Homosexuality is a tough topic, especially because, in today's culture, homosexuality has moved from being a moral issue to a civil rights issue.

THE SHIFT OF CATEGORIES IN THE HOMOSEXUAL CONVERSATION

Instead of framing a conversation around identifying what's truth and what's not, our culture has shifted to focus on total acceptance versus bigotry. For example, on 2008's election night in Chicago, soon-to-be-president Barack Obama began his speech by addressing different groups of people. All of the comparisons are amoral, meaning without moral consequence, except one: "... young and old, rich and poor, Democrat and Republican, black, white, Hispanic, Asian, Native American, gay, straight, disabled and not disabled."[20] This shift from a moral issue to a civil rights issue states that our personal lifestyles dictate truth. "Who can say what is right for the rest of us?" is the mantra of the day. The newly elected president's descriptors were intended to describe a broad net of the American identity—most of which were true at birth or amoral.

Another example of this shift is a North Carolina ad directed toward those voting on the constitutional amendment defining marriage as a union between a man and a woman. The ad's use of imagery—invoking the Civil Rights Movement of the '50s and '60s— depicts the use of separate water fountains labeled "Straight" and "Gay."[21] This clearly illustrates the point that our society has shifted to seeing moral issues as a matter of civil rights. Previously, civil rights were based on amoral issues like gender equality, age or racial discrimination, or physical handicaps—things that aren't right or wrong. But as we've seen in the five coffee cups, the impact of homosexuality is vastly different than the color of your skin.

In recent years, the debate has shifted even further to not allowing right or wrong to be addressed. This has made an honest conversation on homosexuality very difficult to have without someone being accused of intolerance or hate. My hope is that we can have a clear and compassionate conversation about this subject in order to share the love of Jesus.

In your thinking, is homosexuality primarily a moral issue or a civil rights issue? Why?

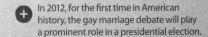

In 2012, for the first time in American history, the gay marriage debate will play a prominent role in a presidential election.

What are the differences between those two ways to approach the conversation?

No matter how you approach the political debates regarding homosexuality, all Christians are called to love God and love others (see Matthew 22:36-40).

A CHRISTIAN'S RESPONSE TO HOMOSEXUALITY

My Aunt Cheryl, Uncle Bobby's sister, has a Bible with this name on the cover: "Robert Lee." These words are handwritten on the first page: "Given to Uncle Robert by Gregg Matte on June 10, 1991."

After I became aware of my uncle's sexual orientation and diagnosis of AIDS, I decided to send him a Bible. I was a youth intern at Hampton Road Baptist Church in Desoto, Texas, making a whopping $100 per week. But I knew I wanted my uncle to have the best Bible I could find—knowing he appreciated the finer things in life, like Porsche 911's. So I delightfully bought the leather bound version and had his name embossed on the bottom right-hand corner. Most importantly, I wanted him to know that the words inside that Bible could change his life. So I sent him the Bible and I told him I was praying for him.

A few months later I got a phone call from Uncle Bobby. He said: "Gregg, thank you for the Bible, but it made me very uncomfortable. I want you to know I will not be reading it." Dejected but trying to sound upbeat, I said: "That's OK, but I want you to know that I love you, and the Bible and Jesus Christ have changed my life. Now you have a copy and can read it anytime you like." Toward the end of his life, Uncle Bobby befriended a priest for guidance and returned to church for a time of confession. His Bible contained markings and underlines, indicating that in fact he had been reading.

As Bobby lay on his deathbed, Aunt Cheryl and her husband, Taylor, sensed the Holy Spirit's prompting to begin reading the Bible to him. The next four days he miraculously remained alive, hearing page after page of God's Word. Uncle Bobby heard the gospel as my aunt and uncle told him: "You can still ask Jesus to be your Savior. He loves you. He'll forgive you. He's not mad at you. He's calling out to you, and He wants you to know Him even in these last moments of your life." My hope is somewhere on the journey Uncle Bobby turned his heart to Jesus.

If you're a Christian heterosexual, how have you responded to homosexuals in the past? Would you change anything if you could?

As we close this session, I want to issue a call for those of us who are Christians to be compassionate Bible-senders, those who weep for people in pain. Let's be broken-hearted revivalists rather than outraged moralists. We must always remember that God loves all of us sinners. Consider what the Book of Romans says about our own sin:

> **"But God demonstrates his own love for us in this: While we were still sinners, Christ died for us" (Romans 5:8).**

Let's love and encourage those around us, fleeing from the attitudes and actions that have gained us the reputations of homophobic hatemongers. I like the way Ed Stetzer, author, speaker, and president of LifeWay Research, summarizes this in a recent blog post:

> "We can, indeed, show grace and friendship to those who struggle, while believing and teaching what the Scriptures clearly say. Without hiding our beliefs, we need to look for opportunities to have conversations, build relationships, and show grace."[22]

If you're personally struggling with homosexuality, understand that Jesus Christ loves you and has so much more in store for you than you can imagine. Turn your heart to Him, and He'll meet you where you are.

> **"I am not ashamed of the gospel, because it is the power of God for the salvation of everyone who believes" (Romans 1:16).**

I encourage you to share your struggle with a trusted Christian counselor or minister. He or she can pray with and encourage you tremendously as you seek God's will for your life. It will most likely be a long and difficult road, but God will lead you to the "more" of His will.

Based on what you've read from the Bible, how should the church relate to those struggling with homosexuality? How should individual Christians respond?

How has this session helped your understanding of God's plan for sexuality?

 If you struggle with homosexuality and need guidance, go to *exodusinternational.org* for more information and help.

APPLY TO LIFE

> **CONNECT:** This week, seek out and connect with several people you respect. Ask them about their views on homosexuality, their understanding of our culture's views, and what our response should be as followers of Jesus.

Also make an effort to connect with at least one homosexual person this week. This doesn't have to be a deep conversation or debate. Just spend some time getting to know your neighbor so that you can love your neighbor.

> **LISTEN:** Purchase "The Struggle" by Tenth Avenue North and "The Hurt & The Healer" by MercyMe (see the playlist at *threadsmedia.com/birdsandbees*). Add these to your regular mix of music throughout the week in order to continue thinking and praying about the issue of homosexuality.

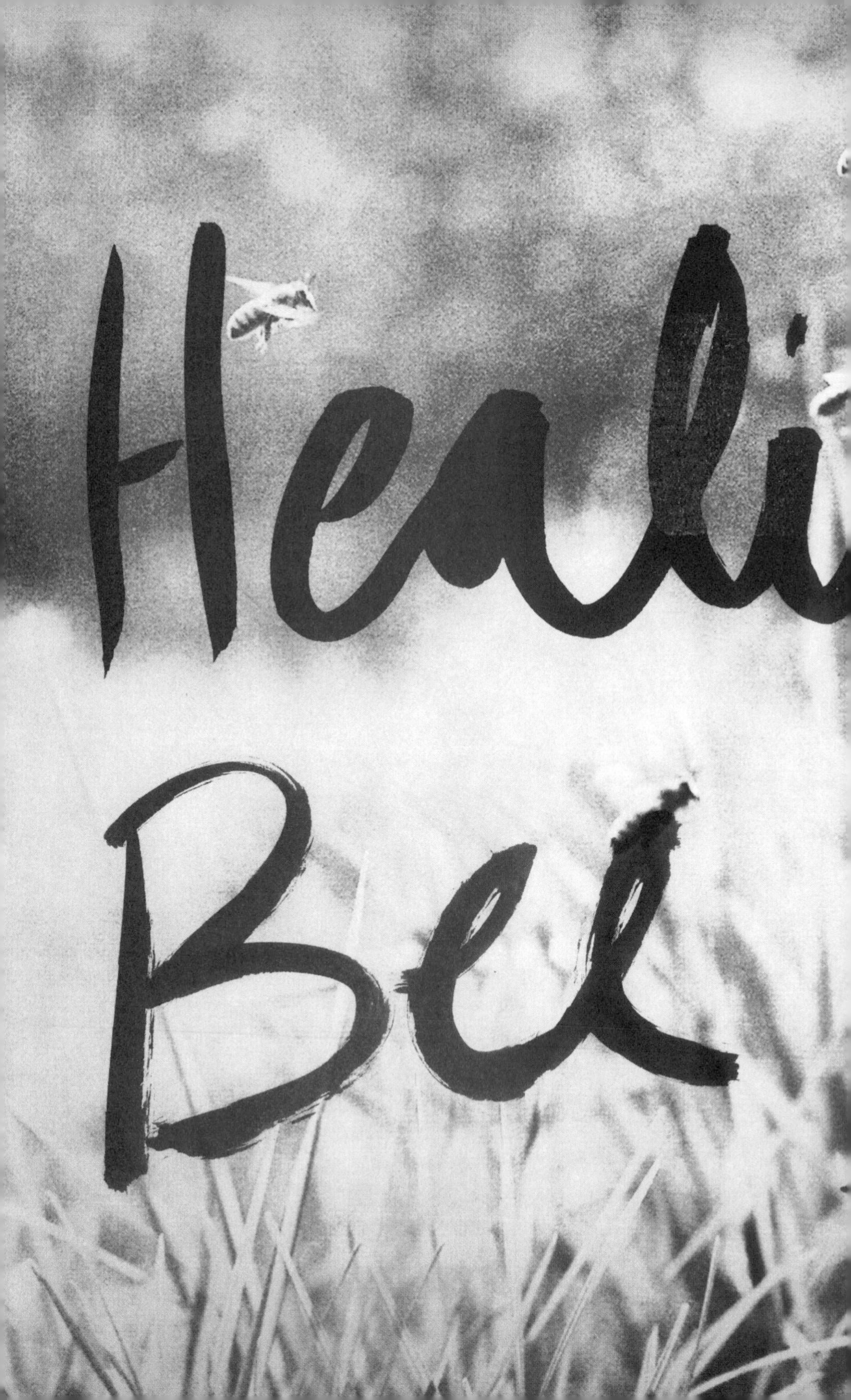
Heali
Bee

I know a lot of guys who played high school and college football. They are different in many ways—old and young, big and small, quiet and loud—but connected by a set of shared experiences and memories they still carry around. They all remember how it feels to push your body to the limit (and sometimes beyond) in an effort to be the best. They remember the thrill of victory and the agony of defeat. Some guys enjoy retelling stories of the "glory days." And the older they get, the better the stories become.

A common denominator reaching even beyond the memories are the injuries. Football is a violent sport, after all. Most injuries are minor—sprains, bruises, cuts—but there are major injuries, too. Sometimes it's easy to spot the evidence of an old injury through a scar. Maybe a guy's finger juts out in the wrong direction, for example. Or he's got a six-inch scar on his knee after surgery to repair a torn ligament. Yet sometimes the evidence stays below the surface, like when a guy limps when the weather turns cold because his ankle swells up.

When people experience trauma, they carry the evidence whether it's seen or unseen. The deeper and more serious a wound, the longer and more powerful the impact.

What were the most serious physical injuries you sustained growing up?

How did those injuries impact you in the short term? The long term?

Just like former football players carry around the evidence of physical injuries, those of us who've been wounded sexually also carry around scars. We're still affected by them—especially if we never truly healed in the first place. Emotional wounds cut far deeper than physical ones. Essentially, there are no minor injuries when it comes to sex and sexuality. Sex is a powerful force, and it always affects us in a powerful way—for good or ill. Whether our wounds are the result of our own choices or of the decisions of those around us, all wounds require healing.

In terms of sex and sexuality, what wounds have you received from others?

 Watch the *Birds and Bees* video for Session 5, available at *threadsmedia. com/birdsandbees.com*.

What wounds do you possess as a result of your own choices?

So let's get started. First, we'll look at receiving spiritual healing through Jesus. Then we'll look at practical ways to address particular wounds from both the past and the present.

JESUS IS THE SALVE FOR OUR WOUNDS

None of us are holy when it comes to sex and sexuality. We haven't behaved completely honorably, and we all have been scathed by our culture and the actions of others. In other words, we each have scars and are in need of healing. So for those of us who are wrapped in a blanket of guilt, we're headed to hope.

Thankfully, we can receive the healing we need through Jesus Christ. Look again at 1 Corinthians 6:

> **"Do you not know that the wicked will not inherit the kingdom of God? Do not be deceived: Neither the sexually immoral nor idolaters nor adulterers nor male prostitutes nor homosexual offenders nor thieves nor the greedy nor drunkards nor slanderers nor swindlers will inherit the kingdom of God. And that is what some of you were.** *But you were washed, you were sanctified, you were justified in the name of the Lord Jesus Christ and by the Spirit of our God"* **(vv. 9-11, emphasis mine).**

If you're kicking yourself for your past mistakes, hear my heart: It doesn't matter what you did in the past that caused you to become wounded—that's what you *were*. That's in the past, and through Christ your past can be made pure. Your future has incredible possibilities. Personally, I've been forgiven for the "bee stings" in my life, and consequently, I now walk confidently in God's grace.

The apostle Peter said something similar in 1 Peter 2:

> **"He himself bore our sins in his body on the tree, so that we might die to sins and live for righteousness; by his wounds you have been healed. For you were like sheep going astray, but now you have returned to the Shepherd and Overseer of your souls" (vv. 24-25).**

What words from the verses above strike you as poignant or powerful? Why?

 Listen to "No Shame" by Moriah Peters, "Reason to Sing" by All Sons & Daughters, and "Love Doesn't Last Too Long" by The Weepies from the *Birds and Bees* playlist, available for purchase at *threadsmedia.com/birdsandbees*.

The same is true for those of us who've been wounded by others. If you've been abused or taken advantage of, you've had a burden unfairly thrown on your shoulders. If you've been scarred by divorce or battered and bruised by a culture that wields sexuality like a hammer, you feel the weight.

But you can find relief. Jesus said:

> "Come to me, all you who are weary and burdened, and I will give you rest. Take my yoke upon you and learn from me, for I am gentle and humble in heart, and you will find rest for your souls. For my yoke is easy and my burden is light" (Matthew 11:28-30).

Jesus Christ died on the cross to reconcile all the times we don't honor God—and all the times we're innocently affected by others who don't honor God. His body was broken and His blood was shed so it could wash over us and forgive what we *were*—past tense. He was wounded so we could be healed.

Therefore, the first question you need to answer to heal your wounds is this: Have you realized and received the good news that Jesus offers forgiveness and embodies the power to live a godly life? Salvation in Christ results in both the cleansing of sin and also the indwelling of the Holy Spirit. Jesus lives inside of you as the source of power over sin. Jesus is the door through which you can find healing, but He's also so much more. Jesus is the only way to find the life God created you to live.

How would you describe your current relationship with Jesus?

What steps can you take now to experience Him more fully as your Savior and Lord?

Here's the second question you need to answer: Are you living as if you've been healed and empowered? Even when we know Jesus, we sometimes continue to live as if we're defined by what happened in the past. We still walk with a limp and drift away from God's plan in the present, even though our wounds have been restored.

For that reason, we'll spend the remainder of this session focusing on specific wounds

----

 If you'd like to learn more about salvation through Jesus Christ, read through the following Bible verses and talk with a minister: Romans 3:23; 5:8; Ephesians 2:8-9; Romans 6:23; Romans 10:9-10; John 3:16.

connected with sex and sexuality—both past and present—and practical steps we can take to embrace the healing we've already received.

PAST WOUNDS

Let's start with the past. Young people, especially children, are incredibly vulnerable. They need to be protected. But it's a great tragedy that so many people have been wounded in so many horrible ways—parental abuse, abandonment, divorce, or rape, to name a few. Wounds inflicted in childhood can haunt a person for the rest of his or her life. Let's examine some common wounds.

Divorce

One of the most pervasive wounds comes from a child's parents dissolving a bond that was supposed to be permanent. My wife has an incredibly strong and close-knit family. Her parents remained married until her mom went to heaven, truly living out "until death do us part." Additionally, her family has lived and ranched on the same land for more than 150 years. They've lived in the same house for more than 100 years, and—true story—one of her ancestors was born in the dining room! Their roots of faithfulness and commitment run deep.

My story is the opposite. Remarriage and divorce is commonplace. Both sets of my grandparents have been divorced, and my parents' marriage split when I was 2 years old. My parents are both great people and have blessed me immensely, but after four years they went separate ways. Divorce is all I knew growing up, and there are scars in my life. "What's best for the parents is best for the kids" is a fallacy. The parents' happiness may increase as they regain singlehood but the child's doesn't. In truth, the dissolution of a marriage has negative affects on the children. Divorce is not a solution to problems; it's an exchange of problems. New fears and baggage enter the kids' backpacks for life. When I started seriously considering marriage, I found out pretty quickly that I was carrying a lot of extra luggage. *Would our marriage make it? What kind of husband would I be? Could I love deeply when I feared it wouldn't last?*

I'm not the only one. Since 1972, more than a million children each year have seen their parents divorce.[1] Think about that for a second: a million children every year. That means tens of millions of kids in recent decades—including the decades when you and I were growing up—have matured in homes where their parents lived under separate roofs.

Maybe you were one of those kids or maybe you'll marry one. Possibly both of these statements are true.

How have you been affected by the prevalence of divorce in recent decades?

 There's still hope for reversing the divorce trend. In 2011, the U.S. Census Bureau found divorce rates for most age groups have been dropping since 1996 by an average of about 5 percentage points.[2]

In your experience, what impact has the prevalence of divorce had on today's culture?

What evidence do you see of that impact?

The Bible has much to say about divorce and its impact on the family. Here are a few verses:

> "Therefore what God has joined together, let man not separate" (Mark 10:9).

> "I tell you that anyone who divorces his wife, except for marital unfaithfulness, and marries another woman commits adultery" (Matthew 19:9).

> "And if she divorces her husband and marries another man, she commits adultery" (Mark 10:12).

> "He who brings trouble on his family will inherit only wind, and the fool will be servant to the wise" (Proverbs 11:29).

Divorce changes everything.

Divorce distorts roles within the family, for one thing. When parents split up, their child is often forced to step up as a caregiver—the child comforting her parents instead of receiving comfort herself. She becomes mantled with being the family peacemaker when her parents argue. As things evolve and her parents begin dating others, the child approves of their dates instead of them approving hers. How odd to wait on the couch for your parent to come home and be asked, "So what do you think? Do you like him/her?"

Parental divorce can alter personalities and the way people approach the world. Children of divorce are hit with a flood of negative feelings and emotions when their parents break up—anger, uncertainty, instability, rejection, anxiety, guilt, and depression. Many children suppress their feelings or seek avenues of escape, often leading to troubled experiences in youth and adulthood. Many turn to drugs and alcohol as a method of numbing their pain and anger. Others turn to sex for intimacy, to fill a parental void, to seek attention, or to help them feel loved or wanted. Many teenagers use sex to inflict pain on their parents as a form of retaliation or to assert their premature independence.

....

 For an in-depth look at the experiences of children of divorce, read *The Unexpected Legacy of Divorce* by Judith S. Wallerstein.

SESSION FIVE BIRDS AND BEES

Living with divorce very often affects a child's view of God. Many kids see their parents' relationship as the "forever thing" in their lives—the one thing that will never change. And if that relationship ends, they begin to question, *Does anything last forever? Is there anyone, including God, who will always be there for me?*

Family is intended to illustrate our relationship with God. Divorce skews those impressions, replacing fulfillment with a void. This is especially true if one of the parents becomes distant. The child subconsciously believes: *If Dad lives apart from me, then the Heavenly Father must be distant as well.* Or, *If I wasn't good enough to keep Mom from leaving, how will I ever be good enough to convince God to stay with me?*

What are other consequences of divorce within a child's life?

How would the consequences you listed affect a child's view of sex and sexuality as he or she grows up?

Be encouraged; there is hope. God can mend what others have torn. In a weird way, my divorced home has increased my commitment to my wife, Kelly, and our kids. Having lived it, I now strongly guard against it.

Clearly, growing up with divorce creates an uphill battle for approaching marriage and sex in a normal way. If that's your situation, it may always be difficult. There are challenges unique to every situation that you have to work through and move beyond. But you can move forward. This was expressed well by David in Psalm 27:

> "Hear my voice when I call, O LORD; be merciful to me and answer me. My heart says of you, 'Seek his face!' Your face, LORD, I will seek. Do not hide your face from me, do not turn your servant away in anger; you have been my helper. Do not reject me or forsake me, O God my Savior. Though my father and mother forsake me, the LORD will receive me" (vv. 7-10).

If you're affected by parental divorce, how can you find encouragement in David's words?

As I mentioned earlier, the first step to moving forward is spiritual healing. It's turning to Jesus as the salve for your wounds. Like David said, you call out to Him and seek His face. It means trusting Jesus to reveal your weaknesses and bring healing. It's turning over your burdens to Him and asking Him to help you in ways no one else can.

Additionally, counseling can be a beneficial experience. A professional counselor can help you identify and work through the long-term repercussions of being a child of divorce.

It's equally important for you to be honest with yourself about your wounds. I remember kneeling after college, my face resting on the cushions of a hand-me-down couch, pouring out my heart to the Lord. It was like the floodgates broke that night. I was honest before God about what I'd been carrying around because of my parents' divorce. And that honesty with myself and the Lord allowed me to rise to my feet and walk stronger.

If you're married, you also need to be honest with your spouse. Kelly and I came from vastly different homes, and we had several conversations about our different assumptions and expectations for our own marriage. Those weren't always fun conversations, but they were essential for us to move forward as one.

Regardless of what you've experienced through divorce, remember to focus on hope rather than fear. You don't have to be a statistic. You don't have to experience the same failures as your parents. Through Jesus, your future has great possibilities. If you're the product of divorce, please don't self-medicate with sex; trust Jesus to be the doctor of healing.

> **"On hearing this, Jesus said, 'It is not the healthy who need a doctor, but the sick'" (Matthew 9:12).**

What are the signs and symptoms of a person who uses sex to self-medicate?

If you're a child of divorce, how can you use that experience to fuel positive relationships in your future?

Abuse
According to the American Academy of Child and Adolescent Psychiatry, there are more than 80,000 incidents of child sexual abuse reported every year in the United States.[3] Obviously, that's 80,000 incidents too many, but it gets worse: Most incidents of child sexual abuse are never reported at all.

Unfortunately, the possibility for sexual abuse doesn't end in childhood. In the United States, a sexual assault occurs every two minutes. Thirty-eight percent of rapists are a friend or acquaintance of their victim.[4] It's estimated that every year, one in eight women in college is raped.[5] Eighty percent of rape and abuse victims are under the age of 30. And unbelievably, 97 percent of rapists will never serve a day in jail.[6]

Sexual abuse is our terrible reality, a heartbreaking reminder of how far mankind has strayed from God's plan for sex and sexuality.

If you've been a victim of abuse, my heart breaks for you. I weep with you. Sexual abuse is a negation of trust. Someone who likely was supposed to love you, hurt you. A trusted family member or friend leveraged time alone for selfish, sinful desires and wounded you.

It's not only that sexual abuse happened; it's the residual shame of feeling like you could've done something to stop the abuse. But no matter what happened to you, you should feel no shame; if you've experienced abuse, you are not at fault. This is described well in Justin Holcomb and Lindsey Holcomb's book *Rid of My Disgrace:*

> "The Bible uses many emotionally charged words to describe shame: reproach, dishonor, humiliation, and disgrace. Additionally, there are three major images for shame in Scripture: nakedness, uncleanness or defilement, and being rejected or made an outcast. These images reflect the experiences of many victims regarding the effects of sexual assault."[7]

And possibly worse, most perpetrators go on with life while you're left to pick up the pieces. I'm sorry for what has happened to you. Your healing, though painful as it may be, provides freedom that you can eventually share with others who are hurting.

Allow God's Word to guide you to healing:

> **"For he has rescued us from the dominion of darkness and brought us into the kingdom of the Son he loves, in whom we have redemption"** **(Colossians 1:13-14a).**

> **"Life will be brighter than noonday, and darkness will become like morning. You will be secure, because there is hope; you will look about you and take your rest in safety. You will lie down, with no one to make you afraid, and many will court your favor" (Job 11:17-19).**

 For free and confidential help available 24/7 in the United States, call the National Sexual Assault Hotline at 1.800.656.HOPE.

> "To you, O LORD, I lift up my soul; in you I trust, O my God. Do not let me be put to shame, nor let my enemies triumph over me. No one whose hope is in you will ever be put to shame, but they will be put to shame who are treacherous without excuse" (Psalm 25:1-4).

A major part of your healing will center on two words: *hope* and *forgiveness*.

Hope is based in the fact that through Christ the future can be different than the past. True love is possible. Cleansing of the mind and heart are available. The wounds can be restored, and righteous justice will be served—this side of heaven or the other.

The second word can be hard for many to hear. But once you've personally received the forgiveness of Jesus, it's important for you to extend that forgiveness to others. Specifically, it's important for you to forgive the one(s) who caused your wounds. Let me hasten to say, this is not letting that person off the hook, lessening the magnitude of the sin, or negating legal action.

Forgiveness doesn't have to be—and likely shouldn't be—face-to-face. The person who wounded you may never be aware. But you need to offer forgiveness in your mind and heart for your own good. The bitterness is hurting you; it's holding you back from what God has planned for you.

Forgiveness doesn't have to be instantaneous. It doesn't have to be today or this moment. I'm talking about a life-long process. As Jesus has forgiven you, offer forgiveness to them. Resentment, hatred, and unforgiveness are poisons that will only cause more wounds if you choose to harbor them into your future. It has been said, "Resentment is drinking poison and waiting for the other person to die." All of us are in need of restoration to some degree, but even more so, it's necessary for those who've experienced the theft of their innocence.

Obviously, this is a subject in which volumes, not paragraphs, of attention are needed. Trust though, with this short mention, that God has declared He loves you, and He is ready and solely able to guide you in your journey to healing. I strongly encourage you to continue the conversation with Him and with a trusted friend or counselor.

How can shame and mistrust from an abusive past keep someone from pursuing healthy relationships?

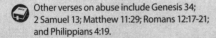
Other verses on abuse include Genesis 34;
2 Samuel 13; Matthew 11:29; Romans 12:17-21;
and Philippians 4:19.

If you haven't been affected by sexual abuse, it's likely that someone close to you has been. Take a few moments to lift these people up in prayer.

Unfaithfulness

The act of unfaithfulness is perhaps the most intimate betrayal a person can endure. If you've ever been cheated on—whether in a serious dating relationship or in your marriage—the deception can deeply wound you. Someone who professed love for you broke your trust and violated the purity of your commitment to one another. Will you ever love and trust again?

Within a marriage, an affair violates a pledge, a vow, made before God. That vow represents a physical, emotional, and spiritual union. Two people have committed to forging through the good and the bad, the unpredictable and the expected together. Their pledges to each other literally made them one:

> "For this reason a man will leave his father and mother and be united to his wife, and the two will become one flesh" (Ephesians 5:31).

What does "the two will become one flesh" mean to you?

When you make a commitment to someone, you expect that the other person will equally honor that covenant. Yet, research shows that at least 22 percent of men and 14 percent of women have had sex outside their marriages.[8] Given the secrecy of this sin, it's hard to say exactly how often infidelity occurs. However, statistics aren't what matters in your relationship. Your significant other made foolish decisions that have brought you grief, shame, and distrust. That's what matters.

> "But a man who commits adultery lacks judgment; whoever does so destroys himself" (Proverbs 6:32).

> "Marriage should be honored by all, and the marriage bed kept pure, for God will judge the adulterer and all the sexually immoral" (Hebrews 13:4).

How does unfaithfulness destroy both the betrayer and the betrayed?

You can survive unfaithfulness. Countless couples have walked through the valley of betrayal and come out stronger as a result, finding forgiveness, restoration, and hope.

If you are the betrayer, first repent and seek forgiveness from God, from your spouse, and eventually, from yourself. What may have taken little time to create will take much longer to resolve. Allow space and time for healing. Commit to restoring your relationship by severing all contact with anyone or anything that tempts you to cheat. You must commit moment-by-moment to being faithful. Another element of restoring honor and respect to your relationship is to answer truthfully your spouse's questions about your betrayal. These conversations will not be fun or easy for anyone involved, but they are essential for moving forward and letting go of the past.

What's the best way to seek reconciliation when you have wronged someone? Include reconciliation with God and others in your answer.

If you were the one betrayed, ask God to guide you in releasing blame and anger toward your spouse. Again, this takes time, but in order for your relationship to be restored, you must come to a place of true, no-strings-attached forgiveness. Secondly, ask questions that require answers, but understand that some things are better left in the past. Consider how much you really need to know and how that information will help you heal. Third, with time, allow your spouse the opportunity to regain your trust. If your relationship is going to survive, your confidence and vulnerability must be restored. This does not mean you must tolerate future indiscretions or deception. Finally, know that it can take years to recover from the emotional impact of infidelity. Allow yourself time to be angry, to grieve, to forgive, to trust once again, and ultimately, to heal.

What insecurities and trust issues develop from being cheated on?

How can unfaithfulness in a dating relationship cause future trust issues for the betrayed person?

When you've been deceived by someone you love, the wounds cut deep. If you're not yet married but have experienced unfaithfulness in a dating relationship, take time to acknowledge and recover from the damage that may have caused you. It's reasonable to think your expectations for and ability to love purely again have been marred. Seek healing from the One who is always faithful.

Another lasting scar of indiscretion could be the result of your parents. You can also survive unfaithfulness between your parents. This also blurs our view of sex and marriage. The tear of infidelity between your parents is difficult to endure, but allow it to strengthen the importance you place on your own purity.

> **"For the word of the LORD is right and true; he is faithful in all he does"** **(Psalm 33:4).**

> **"O LORD, hear my prayer, listen to my cry for mercy; in your faithfulness and righteousness come to my relief" (Psalm 143:1).**

> **"No temptation has seized you except what is common to man. And God is faithful; he will not let you be tempted beyond what you can bear. But when you are tempted, he will also provide a way out so that you can stand up under it" (1 Corinthians 10:13).**

How can God's forgiveness, love, and mercy heal the wounds of unfaithfulness?

Bad Decisions

I've made a distinction so far in this session between sexual wounds caused by others and those we inflict on ourselves. Divorce, abuse, and unfaithfulness are big ones in the first category. But for most of us, the bee stings we've experienced are the direct result of our own choices.

Here's a common story: Boy meets girl and feelings escalate. He's been in several relationships in the past, but this one's different, special. It's so special, in fact, that he considers what it would be like to spend the rest of his life with her.

That's a good story, right? We see it played out in movies all the time. But in real life, however, many men now find themselves face-to-face with their past decisions—often having crossed over the line of appropriate physical intimacy. If the new and special relationship is to progress, they must open the door to an honest and painful conversation about their past sexual decisions. (I'm not picking on guys here. Plenty of young women have a similar story to tell.)

 "There are multitudes of things I would love to have the chance to do over. Now it is quite possible that with a second chance, I would make the same foolish mistakes, but I'd still like the chance to try." —R. C. Sproul, *The Holiness of God*[9]

What experiences have you had with this kind of painful conversation?

What worries you about future conversations on that topic?

Here's another common story: A woman has sex with her boyfriend for the first time. She didn't plan on it, but it happened in a moment of passion and weakness. Now she feels guilty—deeply ashamed because she knows God's plan for sex and she'd always dreamed of saving herself for marriage. The more she thinks about what happened, the more she feels like she's lost her chance at purity. Soon she and her boyfriend have sex again. She still feels guilty about it, but not as much as before. She's already sinned; she's already failed God and failed her future husband—so what's the point of pursuing purity when it's lost forever?

How would you respond to that last question?

Do you believe once a person has sex, purity is "lost forever"? How does Isaiah 1:18-20 speak to this?

Please hear me on this: It's never too late to choose purity. It's never too late to turn back to God and submit once again to His plan for sex and sexuality. If you made a mistake—or many mistakes—the absolute worst thing you can do is continue to make choices that distance you from God. It'll only bring you additional heartache and shame.

We all make bad decisions, and for many of us that includes decisions connected with sexual activity. So how do we move forward?

We can begin with 2 Corinthians 5:17:

> "Therefore, if anyone is in Christ, he is a new creation; the old has gone, the new has come!"

Jesus died on the cross to pay for your mistakes and for mine. They've been taken care of.

 Take a moment to consider how you might approach a difficult conversation with a potential spouse who has made poor choices.

Even better, we're not defined by our past mistakes, because we're no longer the same people. Our "old" selves are gone. Now we get to live as something "new." In other words, we're offered a new virginity through the forgiveness of Jesus—a new chance to choose purity instead of the impurity of the world.

That new chance can start today, if you want. This can be the first moment in a future where you follow God's plan for sex and sexuality—a future filled with great possibilities for healing and fulfillment.

Why is shame so powerful?

Do you truly believe God forgives and cleanses us? How does that make you feel?

Have you ever considered the gospel's power to redeem your sexual failures? How does this change your view of yourself? Of God?

PRESENT WOUNDS

Past failures are just that, in the past. There's nothing we can do to change what has already happened. But unfortunately, not all bad decisions are consigned to the distant past. We make plenty of mistakes in the present. It's important for us to address some lifestyles that distance us from God's plan for sex and sexuality. Let's look again at one portion of our focal passage:

> **"For God did not call us to be impure, but to live a holy life. Therefore, he who rejects this instruction does not reject man but God, who gives you his Holy Spirit" (1 Thessalonians 4:7-8).**

Now let's explore some habits and habitual sins that regularly produce sexual immorality in our lives.

Mental Lifestyles

A sexually immoral lifestyle begins between our ears, not between the sheets. It takes root in our minds well before our bodies take action. We lust. We fantasize. We get emotionally involved. We act. We reject living "a holy life."

We don't get any points for confining lust to our minds. Jesus made it clear that mental immorality is no better than physical immorality. He explained to His disciples that they are to live set apart from the world:

> "You have heard that it was said, 'Do not commit adultery.' But I tell you that anyone who looks at a woman lustfully has already committed adultery with her in his heart" (Matthew 5:27-28).

Why would Jesus draw attention to the heart in His Sermon on the Mount?

How can we escape impure thoughts?

The first step is to realize you're caught in a trap when your thoughts are unchecked. I appreciate how the writer of Proverbs personifies lust as a temptress on the hunt:

> "With persuasive words she led him astray; she seduced him with her smooth talk. All at once he followed her like an ox going to the slaughter, like a deer stepping into a noose till an arrow pierces his liver, like a bird darting into a snare, little knowing it will cost him his life. Now then, my sons, listen to me; pay attention to what I say. Do not let your heart turn to her ways or stray into her paths. Many are the victims she has brought down; her slain are a mighty throng. Her house is a highway to the grave, leading down to the chambers of death" (Proverbs 7:21-27).

If you're surrounded by situations where your mind habitually turns to lust—pornography, fantasizing, sexting, masturbation, ogling, and so forth—you're in trouble. You're snared in something deadly. And the only way you're going to escape is if you first admit that you're caught. Admit you're in trouble and in need of help.

Confess your sin. Jesus already knows, of course, but confession through prayer is a major step toward healing. Confessing your struggle to another person—a parent or a trusted friend, pastor, or counselor—is helpful for removing temptation and finding restoration:

> "Therefore confess your sins to each other and pray for each other so that you may be healed. The prayer of a righteous man is powerful and effective" (James 5:16).

After you've started the process of spiritual healing, the next step is action—get out of the trap.

What triggers can you identify that tempt you to lust?

The M-Word
We all can agree that our thoughts, if left unchecked, birth action. Similarly, unchecked temptations culminate in sin, and unchecked sexual thoughts and urges can result in masturbation. Though the m-word is uncomfortable to read and embarrassing to discuss, it's an essential topic to address in a study on the birds and the bees. Fueled by lust, it is in essence, sex with self. God's biblical plan for sex is that it should be a selfless sharing between two, not the selfish pleasures of one. This act itself brings a disconnection between emotion and sexual fulfillment.[10] It's typically used for the purpose of feeling, escape, self-medicating, or release instead of increasing the emotional and relational bond within marriage.

Sex in marriage is intended to grow love and commitment while "sex with self" serves only to short circuit God's perfect design. Sex is intended to bring intimacy not just fulfillment. After the temporary fulfillment of masturbation is gone, as a believer, you can bet that guilt and embarrassment are right around the corner. Since the Bible teaches the aim of sex is to deepen relationship, then self-sex is a solitary, feeble substitute for the real thing.

My goal is not to heap guilt on those who struggle but to steer you toward the accurate purposes of sex. The fantasies leading to lust and ultimately the solitary action of the m-word can become addictive and destructive. I encourage those struggling with masturbation to memorize 2 Corinthians 10:5:

> **"We take captive every thought to make it obedient to Christ."**

Obedient thoughts lead to obedient actions.

Secondly, it may be helpful to talk with a mature and trusted friend—not someone to just keep you accountable but someone who'll help you cultivate a life of purity in thought and deed. This person can help you understand the "why" instead of just stopping the "what." Focus on the Family describes it as "a self–soothing behavior."[11] Is there a deeper reason for this self-soothing need?

Finally, when you feel tempted to fulfill your lusts through masturbation, do something completely different. Read the Bible. Run a mile. Do 25 push-ups. Change the channel.

Go outside, pray, or take the proverbial "cold shower." Set yourself up to be victorious. Discover the deeper need and decide now what the appropriate outlet will be to meet it.

Take Action
Earlier we looked at Matthew 5:27-28, where Jesus said lusting in our minds has the same spiritual consequences as lusting with our bodies. Now look at what Jesus said we should do about it:

> **"If your right eye causes you to sin, gouge it out and throw it away. It is better for you to lose one part of your body than for your whole body to be thrown into hell. And if your right hand causes you to sin, cut it off and throw it away. It is better for you to lose one part of your body than for your whole body to go into hell" (Matthew 5:29-30).**

Please don't dismember yourself—that's not what Jesus is advocating. Rather, He's saying we should be as thorough as we can when it comes to escaping the trap of lust physically, mentally, and emotionally.

Look again at the Scripture verses above. What words stand out to you most? Why?

Take a few moments to reflect on your decisions throughout the last few years regarding sex. What positive decisions have you made?

What compromising situations have you allowed yourself to be in? How can those motivate you to make changes?

Here's some bad news: You're never going to fully remove yourself from temptation. Our culture is saturated with sex, and you're going to get hit with opportunities to lust no matter how much you try to avoid them. Having an occasional bad thought is going to happen. We are, in fact, human. But the impurity begins when you allow yourself to indulge that thought, to nurture it in your mind and dwell on it for the sake of pleasure. Recognize the temptation, remove it from your mind, and remind yourself of God's Word—as in Job 31:1:

> **"I made a covenant with my eyes not to look lustfully at a girl."**

Everyone living in today's culture needs to memorize that verse. Purity starts with the eyes and the mind, so be vigilant about what you see and what you dwell on in your thoughts.

What have you found to be effective for avoiding temptation?

What other Scripture verses can be helpful in escaping the trap of lust?

Physical Lifestyles

Traps aren't limited to just our minds. We can also get caught in a lifestyle filled with physical expressions of lust. Maybe it's a series of mistakes with casual partners or a serious relationship with a boyfriend or girlfriend that becomes physical.

Diving into physical intimacy before marriage drags you away from God's plan for sex and sexuality—and other areas of life. Life locked into a cycle of sin overflows into the rest of our journey. A cloudy heart limits clear decisions. Essentially, we're asking for more bee stings when we've built our lives beside the hive.

> **"Let us behave decently, as in the daytime, not in orgies and drunkenness, not in sexual immorality and debauchery, not in dissension and jealousy. Rather, clothe yourselves with the Lord Jesus Christ,** *and do not think about how to gratify the desires of the sinful nature"* **(Romans 13:13-14, emphasis added).**

One of the biggest misconceptions many people have about dating and physical intimacy is that everything hinges on whether or not intercourse happens. We justify our activities by coming close "to the line" and thinking: *We did A, B, and C together, but at least we never had sex.* Deception is wrapped in the feeling that as long as we don't go "all the way," then everything else is fair game.

There are two problems with that way of thinking. First, physical intimacy is like an avalanche—once it gets rolling, it's almost impossible to stop. Physical intimacy creates strong bonds between people, and those bonds usually come with a desire for more physical intimacy. In other words, God designed A, B, and C to lead into sex, not to slam on the brakes just before. Our minds and bodies gather momentum as intimacy progresses. Therefore, we have to be very careful about the snowball rolling downhill and hoping it gently stops halfway down the mountain.

 Augustine (A.D. 354-430) was promiscuous before becoming a man of God. After his conversion, walking along the street he saw up ahead a former mistress. He turned to walk the opposite direction, and she called out, "Augustine, it is I." He responded with quick wit, "Yes, but it is not I."

Second, even if we don't go "all the way," we're still starting the process of giving ourselves away. We're giving our bodies and the depths of who we are away in chunks. Remember, sex is not just something we do—it's a part of who we are. The removal of sex from the essence of who we are, to just being an action we do, is false. This thought is an attempt to justify actions by separating them from the person. Two become one at the deepest heart level, elevating sex past the physical. It's not just an activity but a gift of God. For example, to say, "We ate together," just describes an activity. While to say, "We slept together," is to describe a soulful exchange. While eating is sharing an activity, sleeping with someone is sharing who you are.

What evidence supports the idea that sexual activity is a soulful exchange?

How have you seen this avalanche analogy hold true in other areas of your life? For example, one lie leads to more lies, and so forth.

So if you're in the middle of a physical relationship that's gone too far, how do you stop? How can you escape from the trap? The process is similar to escaping from the trap of lust. The first step is to admit you're caught, to confess to God that you haven't followed His plan for sex and sexuality. Repent of your sin and ask for His help.

The next step is to stop doing what you've been doing. You need to stop wounding yourself in order to find deep healing. Removing yourself from the party scene, praying for a different set of godly influences, having a serious conversation with your girlfriend/ boyfriend, or putting a hold on dangerous dating—all of these are small prices to pay to reclaim God's plan. He has more for you than what you're experiencing right now, and His power is strong enough to lead you.

Some of these decisions will be really tough. Like I said, physical intimacy creates strong bonds. But it's necessary if you want to experience God's plan for sex and sexuality. It's part of the "cutting off the hand" I mentioned earlier from Matthew 5.

If you've made mistakes when it comes to physical relationships, keep those mistakes in the past. That's where they belong. You can't change the past, but you can change your trajectory for the future.

How can you protect yourself from making poor decisions in the future?

God created sex to be holy and honorable. He intended us to approach sex and sexuality through a lifestyle of purity so that we can bring glory to Him and experience fulfillment in our own lives. That's the plan. That's the ideal.

Unfortunately, we don't always live up to the ideal. But I want you to understand that even when you make mistakes, you can be forgiven. You can start fresh. Even when you have some serious wounds, you can be healed.

What does a fresh start mean to you?

REMOVING THE STINGER

Before I was a believer in Christ, I got some bee stings myself from following the wild high school crowd. And even after I trusted Christ as my Savior, I made mistakes when I thought going too far was the norm. With those mistakes in my rearview mirror, I'm sorrowful for things gone wrong, but joyous that it feels like a world away, like I was a completely different person. God has brought wonderful, patient, daily change with each step of my walk with Him. He can do the same for you.

Whether you have wounds from someone else's actions or from your own decisions, cling to these verses:

> "Therefore, since we have been justified through faith, we have peace with God through our Lord Jesus Christ, through whom we have gained access by faith into this grace in which we now stand. And we rejoice in the hope of the glory of God. Not only so, but we also rejoice in our sufferings, because we know that suffering produces perseverance; perseverance, character; and character, hope. And hope does not disappoint us, because God has poured out his love into our hearts by the Holy Spirit, whom he has given us. . . . For if, when we were God's enemies, we were reconciled to him through the death of his Son, how much more, having been reconciled, shall we be saved through his life! Not only is this so, but we also rejoice in God through our Lord Jesus Christ, through whom we have now received reconciliation" (Romans 5:1-5,10-11).

How does this passage bring you hope for transformation?

Remember, forgiven bee stings lead to hearing birds sing.

APPLY TO LIFE

> **PRAY:** Pray continually this week that the Holy Spirit will reveal the different wounds you're suffering from—whether or not you're currently aware of those wounds. Pray also for both short-term and long-term healing as you identify each wound.

> **STUDY:** Continue memorizing 1 Thessalonians 4:1-8 by focusing on verses 7-8: "For God did not call us to be impure, but to live a holy life. Therefore, he who rejects this instruction does not reject man but God, who gives you his Holy Spirit."

> **READ:** As part of your Bible study this week, look for passages of Scripture that talk focus on healing or being healed. (You can get a great list of passages to read by doing a word search for "heal" on *mystudybible.com*.) Look for patterns by keeping the following questions in mind as you read through the verses:

1. Who needs healing?
2. Who provides healing?
3. What are the methods of healing?

Hearir

Bird

Sin

Sex is powerful. Not many people would dispute that statement given the impact in our lives and in the culture as a whole. But even when we recognize that power, we're still left with an important question: Will it be used for good or evil? Building us up or tearing us down?

God designed sex to be a powerful force for our good. Sex is the most intimate experience two humans can share. In the proper context, it can build incredibly strong bonds and bring physical pleasure. It's amazing to ponder that a single sexual experience has the potential to produce life, which can kindle an entire family tree of lives—generation after generation of people created in God's image.

Unfortunately, sex can also be a powerful force for our harm. When God's plan is rejected or ignored, we open ourselves to physical, emotional, and relational repercussions—bee stings—that can last a lifetime. Ultimately, our choices determine whether our experiences result in great blessings, as God intended, or in great pain.

Up to this point in your life, have your experiences with sex and sexuality resulted in more blessings or trials? Why?

We've been talking about the birds and the bees throughout this study, and I doubt anyone reading this has been able to avoid all the bee stings we discussed in previous sessions. We've all been wounded. But we don't have to settle for those experiences, and we don't have to continue the cycles of sin.

LIVING IN THE BLESSING GOD INTENDED

Earlier in the study I highlighted two words, *holy* and *honorable,* to explain God's design for sex and sexuality. We looked at another pair of words, *excess* and *access,* to explore our culture's current views on the topic. Let's focus now on two additional words that serve as the foundation for fulfilling sex within the context of a marriage.

Giving
How do you experience wonderful, godly intimacy? It's all about giving instead of getting. We get a sense of this from 1 Corinthians 7:3-5:

> **"The husband should fulfill his marital duty to his wife, and likewise the wife to her husband. The wife's body does not belong to her alone but also to her husband. In the same way, the husband's body does not belong to him alone but also to his wife. Do not deprive each other except by mutual**

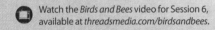 Watch the *Birds and Bees* video for Session 6, available at *threadsmedia.com/birdsandbees*.

consent and for a time, so that you may devote yourselves to prayer. Then come together again so that Satan will not tempt you because of your lack of self-control."

What words stand out to you from those verses?

Take a moment to concisely rewrite these verses in your own words. What do they communicate about a healthy sexual relationship?

Upon marriage, you give yourself away to your spouse. The emotional, spiritual, physical, and practical acts of sharing life with another person are inherently intimate. The man's body no longer belongs to him alone, but to his wife; the woman's body no longer belongs to her alone, but to her husband.

Your body is offered as a gift to your spouse as a physical representation of your commitment and trust. The emotional and spiritual sharing of life and love expresses itself tangibly.

Being together is far more than physical. A couple has given themselves away spiritually, mentally, and emotionally, building trust through shared thoughts, feelings, and commitment. The focus is on blessing your spouse rather than the pleasure you receive. When you're both giving to one another, you both receive.

This is the opposite of how sex is usually portrayed today. Our culture views sex as an opportunity for taking, rather than giving. The Internet, magazines, and TV encourage us to consume whatever we desire to satisfy ourselves. There's no relationship required, no mutual trust or commitment—just selfish passions being served. Feeding fleshly desires never satisfies us or produces fulfillment. Instead it drives us to take more and more in an endless cycle of discontent.

Adultery is a perfect example. It's all about selfishly seeking pleasure, passion, power, a cheap thrill, or attention. Our culture says, "If you're not happy or satisfied with what you've got, go and take something else." But the end result is the shattering of individuals and families—often of multiple families. Unfortunately, there's always a story of infidelity in the headlines screaming, "It wasn't worth it!" As scandals break into the news, absorb them as teachable moments.

....

 Authors Rodney and Selma Wilson, in an article "The Secret to Great Sex," explain that "we all have an inclination to look out for ourselves first. Putting the needs and desires of others first is a daily struggle. That struggle is why Paul died to self daily, striving to be like Christ and get himself out of the way (1 Corinthians 15:31)."[1]

Steve Farrar, in his book *Finishing Strong,* wisely states,

> "Throughout the Bible, there are three inescapable principles concerning sin. . . . Sin will take you farther than you wanted to go . . . keep you longer than you wanted to stay . . . cost you more than you wanted to pay."[2]

Do you agree with Steve Farrar on his view of sin? Why or why not?

When love is based on taking rather than giving, it quickly runs off the rails because it takes advantage of other people. It causes us to wrong others by consuming and hoarding in a spirit of selfishness. But marriage that produces true fulfillment always begins with giving.

What evidence supports that our culture views sex as taking and not giving?

How can we determine whether our desires for sex and sexuality are associated with giving or taking?

Receiving
Giving is the first word that serves as the foundation for fulfilling sex within the context of marriage. The second word is *receiving.* Receiving love is often as complicated as giving love. Clinical counselors and relationship experts Harville Hendrix and Helen LaKelly Hunt (a husband and wife team) have found this to be true in many of their patients:

> "The common wisdom is that romantic relationships would stay happy if people did a better job of giving to each other. But that's not what we've discovered. We've found that many people need to do a better job of receiving the gifts their partners are offering."[3]

Why can receiving love be so difficult?

Listen to "L-O-V-E" by Nat "King" Cole, "Haven't Met You Yet" by Michael Bublé, and "Let's Stay Together" by Al Green from the *Birds and Bees* playlist, available for purchase at *threadsmedia.com/birdsandbees.*

Consider the hurts and hang-ups we often gather on life's journey. Those wounds, many we discussed in Session 5, leave us with protective walls where we insulate ourselves to hedge the risk of being hurt. If there's any place where walls must come down, it's between a husband and wife.

Receiving someone's total love, trust, and commitment can be scary, though. Ironically, what we often desire the deepest—love, acceptance, and connection with a mate—we simultaneously may fear the most. Finding someone to share your life with can automatically generate apprehension that the relationship won't work out, that he wasn't genuine, or that she will leave or otherwise wound you.

What fears do you have about your current or future marriage?

What steps can you take to simultaneously guard yourself for the right person and still be open to having a fulfilling marriage?

A PATH FOR FAITHFULNESS

With giving and receiving as a back drop, let's focus one final time on 1 Thessalonians 4 and Paul's charge to live lives that please God. The Bible gives us a host of guidance for our personal relationships. Specifically, we can learn some practical steps for healthy relationships from three verbs in this passage:

> **"It is God's will that you should be sanctified: that you should avoid sexual immorality; that each of you should learn to control his own body in a way that is holy and honorable, not in passionate lust like the heathen, who do not know God; and that in this matter no one should wrong his brother or take advantage of him. The Lord will punish men for all such sins, as we have already told you and warned you" (vv. 3-6).**

Take a moment to jot down the verbs in these verses. Which ones stand out in connection with sex and sexuality?

What have you learned from these verses during this study?

Know

The first verb I want to highlight is *know*. Paul wrote that the heathens had given into passionate lust because they didn't "know God" (v. 5). So those of us following God's plan for sex and sexuality must work to know Him more and more—and to find our satisfaction in Him.

It all starts with falling in love with Jesus. When we walk with Christ and want to serve and please Him, it elevates every aspect of our lives—including our sexuality. So how do we stay faithful as single men and women? How do we stay faithful as husbands or wives? We get to know God intimately, and we allow Him to meet our needs.

Maybe that sounds strange—having God meet our sexual needs and desires—but satisfaction is more than bodily gratification. God, as our Creator, is the one who completely meets our physical, emotional, and spiritual needs. No human has that ability. God originally gave us yearnings for love and security, longings for intimacy and relationship, and so He alone provides fulfillment. By pursuing Him for our material and emotional needs, we find eternal enrichment of our spiritual needs. Because God is our foundation, we will only find contentment in following His plan.

Speaking of contentment, look at what Paul wrote in Philippians 4:

> "I am not saying this because I am in need, for I have learned to be content whatever the circumstances. I know what it is to be in need, and I know what it is to have plenty. I have learned the secret of being content in any and every situation, whether well fed or hungry, whether living in plenty or in want. I can do everything through him who gives me strength" (vv. 11-13).

Contentment is the fruit of trusting God, and being content is possible with your sexual desires. Be content with where God has placed you. If you're a single adult, God knows your struggles. It is far better to be single wanting to be married, than married wanting to be single. If you're married and desiring to stay faithful to your spouse, God knows. He knows everything you're dealing with, and He can help you find contentment in your situation if you'll submit to following His plan. All we need is found in Him.

Are you currently content with where God has you in life? Why or why not?

 John 3:16 illustrates how Jesus gave His life so that we could receive new life in Him. As part of receiving Christ's gift of salvation, we honor Him by giving our lives to making much of His name.

What would bolster your level of contentment right now?

Avoid

Another verb that stands out is *avoid*. Paul encouraged followers of God to "avoid sexual immorality" (v. 3). In the original Greek language, the word *avoid* carries with it a sense of personal responsibility. Yes, our culture is filled with excess and access when it comes to sexual immorality and lust, but it's our responsibility to actively avoid those temptations. We are the ultimate deciders of what we do.

It's possible to stub your toe, accidentally let a word fly, and think, *Where in the world did that come from?* But nobody ends up naked with another person and says, "Oops, how did this happen?" It's possible to accidentally pull up a pornographic Web site by clicking on the wrong link. But there's nothing accidental about circumventing the Internet filter or erasing your Web history. There are steps involved with lust and immorality that require intentional decisions, and we're personally accountable for making the right choices.

Here's one quick example. As a college student, I quickly figured out that watching TV after midnight gave far more opportunity for lust. The programming and my guard against sin were both very different late into the night. I realized I was far more likely to make a poor decision and give in to lust, so I had to consciously choose not to turn the TV on. I was personally responsible for avoiding that door to immorality. (Now, in my 40s, falling asleep way before midnight solves this problem.)

The same is true for you. You alone have the responsibility of self-examination: Determine what causes you to struggle, and make firm, active decisions based on those realities. The old adage is true, "A person who doesn't want to fall should not walk in slippery places." Will power isn't enough, so set clear boundaries for yourself and rely on the power of the Holy Spirit to guide you to victory.

What situations are most dangerous for you when it comes to lust and sexual immorality? When are you more likely to stumble?

What factors commonly trigger temptation for you? (Consider your emotions, visual stimuli, stress, relational connections, use of alcohol, and so on.)

Write down three specific steps you can take this week that will help you shirk poor decisions. Keep in mind, victory is based on trusting God's strength, not yours.

Here's another practical tip for avoiding lots of trouble, including sexual immorality. It's something I learned from our church's counseling director Adam Mason, but it's also used in other places: the acronym H.A.L.T. Generally speaking, you never want to make decisions when you're **H**ungry, **A**ngry, **L**onely, or **T**ired. Our ability to make the right choice decreases when we experience any of these four symptoms—including decisions of sexual purity.

Learn
The third and final verb I want to highlight is *learn*. Paul told the Thessalonians they needed to "learn to control" their bodies (v. 4). And so do we. Specifically, we need to learn how to control the different urges and desires that often drive sexual immorality.

While it's clear that many people use sex just for sheer pleasure, sex isn't always about sex. There are often deeper desires that drive our choices. People use sex to gain acceptance, love, respect, power, or to feel pretty or wanted. I like what Larry Crabb writes on this topic:

> "Even Christians who really should know better try to relieve *personal* pain with *physical* pleasure. When we hurt from rejection, emptiness, fear, or loneliness, the temptation to gain relief by pleasantly arousing our physical senses is almost irresistible. We snack on potato chips when we're bored, climb into a hot tub when we're tense, masturbate when we feel alone— something, anything to replace the ache in our hearts with good feelings."[4]

So here's a question: In regard to our failures with sex, *What are we really looking for?* Are we looking for relaxation? Are we looking for release? Are we looking for someone to tell us we're important or valuable?

Scottish writer Bruce Marshall cut to the root of this issue when he said, "Every man who knocks on the door of a brothel is looking for God."[5] We use sex as a gateway for many things but the essence of true life is in Christ.

 To better "know God," have a daily quiet time. Read "How to read and study the Bible" by George H. Guthrie at *lifeway.com* to get started.

SESSION SIX **BIRDS AND BEES**

How would you answer the question, *What are we really looking for?*

What desires or past wounds have influenced your answer to this question in recent months?

How can the need you're seeking be met in Christ? (Avoid "churchy" answers here.)

Sexual desire is real, and it's a part of us. But deeper issues are at play and we must remember that those deeper needs—the desire to be valued, cared for, and loved—are ultimately met through our relationship with God. He can heal your physical and emotional pain; a physical act or a mental fantasy cannot. So examine what's going on internally. Sin is a legitimate need met in an illegitimate way. Identify what you are *really* looking for and pursue it within the context of Scripture and a relationship with the Savior, Jesus Christ. The unveiling of deeper desires frees you from sins of lust and false intimacy.

Meeting our needs through Jesus is the route of mastering control of our bodies "in a way that is holy and honorable, not in passionate lust like the heathen, who do not know God" (1 Thessalonians 4:4-5).

What are your legitimate needs? How can you meet those needs at a soul level instead of just in the flesh?

How do you react to learning more and more about God as the way to meet your legitimate needs? Why?

What deeper needs have driven you to seek out physical pleasure in the past?

What steps can you take to satisfy those needs in a healthy and God-honoring way?

SET YOURSELF UP FOR SUCCESS

God created sex and sexuality, and He has a plan leading to our fulfillment and His glory—if we'll choose to follow it. Let's spend some time focusing on practical things we can do to follow His plan—whether we're married or single.

When You're Married

Fulfilling sex is all about giving and receiving, but what can married people do in their day-to-day lives that will enhance their physical and relational intimacy?

1. Grow your marriage daily. Invest time in activities and conversations that result in a deeper and more robust relationship. Time is the key. Be intentional with the time you spend together. Date nights have been a staple in my marriage since the beginning. For 15 years, almost weekly Kelly and I have gone on a date. Use the focused time to evaluate how things are going, what needs to change, and set mutual goals to work toward. Connecting conversationally is the key to connecting physically because verbal depth is a precursor to physical depth.

In your experience, what obstacles prevent married couples from investing time in their relationship?

Which married couples in your life genuinely enjoy spending time with each other? What lessons can you learn from their relationship?

I've found when a couple has trouble moving deeper in their relationship, the problem often boils down to a lack of communication and different definitions of quality time. Oftentimes, men prefer side-by-side conversations while women like talking face-to-face. I like to sit next to my wife and watch a game, for example. In my mind, that's quality time. Take note, men: That doesn't necessarily count in the ladies' minds.

Women are different, and that's good. My wife really enjoys it when we sit across from each other at dinner and talk for an hour or so—especially if we can share important thoughts and emotions we've experienced in recent days.

When a husband and wife don't understand these differences, it can cause a lot of confusion. I remember a time when my wife and I drove from Houston to New Orleans. That's at least a five-hour drive, and we spent the whole time listening to music, making small talk, and looking out the windows as Louisiana passed by. I thought it was great time together.

Later that night my wife said, "I just don't feel like we're spending enough time together." *Enough time together!* I thought we'd just spent multiple hours together in the car! But that was side-by-side time, and Kelly was talking about face-to-face time. Quantity and quality are different. Once I began to understand the difference, the quality of our time together improved—and so did the depth of our relationship. Just being together is not necessarily quality time. The presence of give and take increases the fulfillment of the relationship, which acts as the foundation for intimacy. Distance in the living room will become distance in the bedroom.

Do you prefer side-by-side time or face-to-face time? How does the typical gender difference act as a God-given balance to relationships?

How does that preference show up in your marriage?

2. Understand what makes your spouse feel connected to you. As we explored in Session 2, many men approach sex by crossing a physical bridge first; they respond to physical and visual stimulation. Women typically approach sex by first crossing an emotional bridge; they respond to tenderness and build trust before they're ready to become physically intimate.

The application is simple. Men, we need to approach our wives with tenderness. There needs to be kindness. There needs to be intentional love. We need to speak caring words in the morning and all through the day. Offering genuine hugs and compliments is an expression of giving her the words she needs. I often tell my wife things like, "I'm faithfully yours. You're the only one for me. I would marry you all over again. You're the most beautiful woman in the world." These words are sincere in expressing my love for her, and they build up her heart. They aren't a scheming forerunner to sex but words of affirmation of our marriage.

Guys listen up, there has never been a woman in a marriage counselor's office talking about how her husband told her she was beautiful and he loved her too much. But the contrary is seen every day. Look her in the eye, and shower her with sincere words of love.

At the same time, women need to help their husbands cross the physical bridge by approaching them in a way that's visually and physically exciting. A man's physical bridge is a "wiring" by God and needs to be understood by the wife. Go the extra mile to look pleasing to him. Some ladies will dress for a lunch with their girlfriends but not put on makeup for their husbands. He will appreciate the extra effort on his behalf. Additionally, build him up with your words and actions. It changes a man's perspective on his work and home life when he knows his wife is supporting and encouraging him. It's essential that your husband knows you respect him and trust him—which is primarily shown through your tone and actions. Finally, be intentional about meeting his needs and honoring him.

For men and women, there needs to be a mutual pursuit developed in the context of mutual trust. Helping each other cross their bridges leads to journeying to the other side of the river together. Let's read how Solomon and his bride approached one another:

> "How beautiful your sandaled feet, O prince's daughter! Your graceful legs are like jewels, the work of a craftsman's hands. Your navel is a rounded goblet that never lacks blended wine. Your waist is a mound of wheat encircled by lilies. Your breasts are like two fawns, twins of a gazelle. Your neck is like an ivory tower. Your eyes are the pools of Heshbon by the gate of Bath Rabbim. Your nose is like the tower of Lebanon looking toward Damascus. Your head crowns you like Mount Carmel. Your hair is like royal tapestry; the king is held captive by its tresses. How beautiful you are and how pleasing, O love, with your delights! Your stature is like that of the palm, and your breasts like clusters of fruit. I said, 'I will climb the palm tree; I will take hold of its fruit.' May your breasts be like the clusters of the vine, the fragrance of your breath like apples, and your mouth like the best wine.
>
> *Beloved*
>
> May the wine go straight to my lover, flowing gently over lips and teeth. I belong to my lover, and his desire is for me. Come, my lover, let us go to the countryside, let us spend the night in the villages. Let us go early to the vineyards to see if the vines have budded, if their blossoms have opened, and if the pomegranates are in bloom—there I will give you my love. The mandrakes send out their fragrance, and at our door is every delicacy, both new and old, that I have stored up for you, my lover" (Song of Songs 7:1-13).

 Statistics prove that the first years of marriage are the most difficult. According to the U.S. Census Bureau, first marriages that end in divorce last an average of eight years.[6]

What words or phrases from this passage connect with a physical and emotional approach to sex?

Why do you think God designed marriage this way?

God specifically designed men and women with different needs so that husbands and wives could work together to meet those needs. Building a fulfilling sexual relationship is all about giving and receiving. It's in the endless cycle of give and take that two become one.

What kinds of things does your spouse enjoy that strengthen your relationship?

What kinds of things do you need to tell your spouse you enjoy?

3. Be lovers, not roommates. More than sharing the bills and responsibilities, married couples are sharing their lives. Roommates operate independently while sleeping at the same address. Marriages grow as they operate interdependently, not independently.

A marriage usually begins with a high level of passion and excitement, but then life gets heavier and heavier; it presses down on us from all sides. Jobs, mortgages, and children are blessings but bear a tremendous weight of responsibility leaving us tired and often lazy in our marriages. We simply don't have the strength at the end of the day for conversation, problem solving, or listening to our spouse. In this stage of marriage, the lights going out at night typically means sleep not sex. I remember my married groomsmen talking with the single guys before my wedding. One said, "I know you don't believe it, but some nights you'll just be too tired to have sex." I thought he was crazy. I was a 26-year-old testosterone-filled man just days from a honeymoon.

As I've since discovered, my groomsman was right. The exhaustion and weight of responsibility can be greater than the passion of the relationship at times. It seems like too much work for the husband to write a note of appreciation to his wife, or it costs too much money to buy a spontaneous surprise. The wife feels too tired to pursue her husband in a physical way. If left unchecked the inadvertent actions can tailspin. Fight for your marriage relationally, and you'll see the difference sexually.

Imagine what it would look like for a married couple to live as roommates rather than lovers. What examples would show living as roommates instead of lovers?

Jot down an idea of what you could do to change that if you were in that situation.

Within marriages men usually evaluate their sexual relationship in terms of frequency, whereas women tend to evaluate their sexual relationship in terms of intimacy. If a couple is having sex often (possibly weekly or more), the man is usually satisfied. If sex is an intimate experience that results in a deep connection, women are typically satisfied even if it doesn't happen as often. Regardless of frequency or intimacy, the good news is both men and women can find sex fun, exhilarating, and pleasurable.

God created men and women differently, but those differences actually complement each other. Combining frequency with intimacy results in passion. Just as fire and gasoline are powerful when combined, when sex is both frequent and intimate, it produces flames of passion and a healthy marriage relationship.

How have your expectations about the frequency of sex changed since you were a newlywed? How would your spouse answer that question?

If you're single, what are your expectations in regard to frequency and intimacy?

Why is it important for frequency and intimacy to be unified?

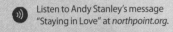

Listen to Andy Stanley's message
"Staying in Love" at *northpoint.org*.

SESSION SIX BIRDS AND BEES

When You're Single

Many of you are single. You haven't been called to act on your God-given sexual desires . . . yet. You have the right urges but wrong timing. Still you are to be a faithful steward of your body, your mind, and your sexuality—all of which God has given you as gifts. You're called to glorify God with your faithfulness just as much as married people glorify God through their sexual expression.

Let me say this right off the bat: That's a challenging job. Faithfully stewarding your sexuality as a single person in today's culture is difficult, and at times, extremely frustrating. For those who are considering sex outside of marriage, hear my heart. Introducing sex into a non-committed relationship only increases the likelihood of a relationship ending. Contrary to popular thought, sex outside of marriage in fact worsens the relationship. It prematurely opens the door to physical and emotional pressures the undeveloped relationship is not able to withstand.

Most of my adult single days were spent leading Breakaway Ministries at Texas A&M. As you can imagine, teachings on dating were always well received by the university students. So I took my waiting on the Lord for a wife to the Scriptures and then to the pulpit. My first and possibly most famous series was entitled "Dating Jesus." The next one, a few years later, continued the theme of loving Christ while waiting, and I called it "Still Dating Jesus." I told a friend if I did another dating series and was still single the title would be "Still Dating Jesus and I'm Ticked Off About It!" So I understand waiting by force not choice. It can be done, and I want to help you prepare for success both now and in the future.

1. Protect your purity. The starting line is cherishing yourself and the gifts God has given you. Everything about you is more valuable than you can imagine—your body, yes, but also your heart, your mind, and your emotions. Guard them. Don't give yourself away visually, emotionally, or physically. In addition, don't take what doesn't belong to you. Purity starts in the eyes and the mind, so be careful about what you see and what you allow your thoughts to dwell on.

> **"Finally, brothers, we instructed you how to live in order to please God, as in fact you are living. Now we ask you and urge you in the Lord Jesus to do this more and more" (1 Thessalonians 4:1).**

How are men and women uniquely called to "please God"?

How does reading that your purity is a gift from God change your view on sex?

Allow me to address the sexes individually for a moment.

To the guys: Our sex-oriented culture places a lot of pressure on men to lust after women. Yet consider what this is doing to the hearts and minds of women. Many men put women in a hypothetical corner, making them feel as though they must have sex in order to earn love. This is communicating to women that their highest value comes through a sexual act. And while the God-given desires within men might lead some to falsely believe such a thing, consider whether or not we would believe that lie about our own mothers, sisters, or even future daughters.

A woman's value and worth is not determined by her physical beauty or sexual prowess. It's rooted in the fact that God created her in His image because He loves her and sent His Son to die for her.

What examples can you give that portray men who view women as objects of sex?

How can a guy treat a lady in a God-honoring way?

And to the ladies, today's culture strongly pushes women to give themselves away visually through the clothes they wear. All types of women have embraced this kind of fashion—young and old, single and married.

Dressing immodestly devalues those who embrace it. You're saying through your clothing: "My figure is the most valuable part of me." Many women have been taught that their bodies can be used as tools to generate attraction and attention and have chosen bad attention over no attention.

You've been handcrafted and designed by God as a gift for your possible future spouse. I urge you to reserve it according to God's plan. You're too valuable to offer yourself in any other way. Though it requires more effort, it is possible to dress fashionably and attractively and still remain classy.

 While the Bible doesn't speak specifically to dating, these Scriptures can provide godly direction as you pursue relationships: Psalm 19:14; Proverbs 3:6; Romans 6:12-13; Galatians 5:13,16; Philippians 4:8-9,13; Colossians 3:5-6.

How does an immodestly-dressed woman devalue herself?

How can a lady honor God with her clothing?

How are men pressured to give themselves away today?

When have you felt pressure to give yourself away in recent months? What was the result?

2. Don't compromise. Hear this loud and clear: Don't rush into a lifelong commitment because you're getting antsy. I'm not saying wait until you find someone perfect. You'll never find that person in life or in the mirror. But you can find someone who's godly. As Paul implied in 1 Corinthians 7:7-8, some are called to marry and some aren't. Don't get so caught up in what you don't have that you miss the blessings of what you do have.

What characteristics would your ideal spouse have? What would be

What characteristics would be "deal-breakers" in a potential spouse?

What blessings can you find and embrace from being single?

3. Prepare your heart and life. When I use the word *prepare,* I'm talking about an active preparation. Become the person you want to marry. If you desire a prayer warrior, pray more. If you desire a spouse who knows the Bible, then read the Word. If faithfulness and truthfulness are high on your list, don't cut corners in your own life.

Before opening yourself up to dating, it's important to establish for yourself some ground rules. Though this wisdom came from a youth minister about 20 years ago, it's still some of the best dating advice around. This acronym is called the "Date Prayer":

Date with good intentions.

Ask God for the right individual to date.

Talk about your dating relationships with an accountability partner.

Expect positive results.

Pray before dates.

Resist temptation by dating with another couple or in groups.

Ask God to build a friendship first and foremost.

Yield to God's timing. It's perfect.

Expect great new relationships to develop.

Relax. God is in control.

Being single can be difficult when our culture accepts and often expects us to have premarital sex. Yet sex isn't the answer for everything. Married or not, there will always be temptations. One 31-year-old single Christian blogger further explained this:

> "Telling people to save sex for marriage is not enough when marriage isn't a guarantee. Chastity is a way of life, looking at our physical, mental, emotional, and spiritual health. It's not solely focused on the physical act of sex. We need to get away from 'how far is too far' and move toward respecting ourselves as men and women made in the image of Christ."[7]

If you're single, know that God has a plan for you. Trust Him to lead you to fulfillment in Him as you maintain purity in His strength.

LOVE LETTERS

I spent a lot of years as a single adult, and as I said, I was "still dating Jesus and ticked off about it" at times. It was honestly a struggle for me. I deeply desired to find my bride and experience all the blessings that come with marriage. With extra time on my hands and an ache in my heart, I prayed. And as I prayed, I watched all of my friends find their special someone. Who knows how many groomsman tuxedos I rented, but I kept praying that God would give me a bride.

I decided to use the time of waiting as a time of preparation, so I began to write letters to my future wife. I was a sophomore in college when I wrote the first one:

 In his book, *Our Unmet Needs*, Charles Stanley observes, "In most cases, marriage is not a need—it is a perceived solution to one or more needs."[8]

Dear ?,

Well it's 2:41 AM on Thursday May 2nd,1990. I should be studying for finals but instead I'm dreaming about you. You ~~take~~ take up "alot" of my time.

I don't know if we've met or not. But I do know that I love you. It's so awesome that God has created us for each other. I don't know what's going on in your life right now but I'm praying for you. And I know you're praying for me.

I love you so much + I don't even know who you are! I'm positive that my life is going to have new meaning with you to share it with.

With Christ our focal point nothing can stop us. He loved us enough to give us each other so we need to give Him our lives.

I'm going to write the words of a song down on the back that is a description of what our marriage will be. No matter what happens know that I love you!

I love you,

Gregg

Eph. 5:25-28

Writing that note seemed to help with the pressure I was feeling, so I kept writing. I wrote note after note after note. I wrote for seven years, and used "Dear ?" to address each note. The "?" was God's business; it was my business to love and be faithful to her before knowing her. Because of the sovereignty of God I was, in a sense, already married. He knew the woman in my future so I decided to honor her in the present. After I finished each letter, I stored them in a box in my closet.

Then something changed on October 10, 1996. At 5:19 p.m., somewhere between Dallas, Texas, and Abilene, Texas, on an American Airlines napkin I wrote:

My waiting turned to receiving and my faithfulness turned to fruition. Love doesn't always happen like that. Yet regardless of whether God provides what we desire, He is still good. Keep trusting Him wherever you are on the journey.

Here's the last note I wrote on our wedding day:

Kelly,   8-2-97 2:41am

This is the completion of my notes. Tomorrow, actually today we will be married. I'm blessed beyond belief to have you. I'm so excited to spend the rest of my life w/you. Kelly you are more than I ever hoped for.

Tonight's dinner was incredible. It couldn't have gone better! Praise Him! I love you.

Your Husband,

Sezz

When we returned from our honeymoon, I gave Kelly my box of letters as a final wedding gift. She sat on the sofa in our new house and bawled her eyes out reading every note, so about three notes in I gave her some space. They touched her deeply to read my words of love long before we had met. Even today, those notes are still cherished, kept in the same box I gave to her.

BRINGING IT TOGETHER

Coming to the end of our study, we've made it through some embarrassing words and uncomfortable concepts. All of our sessions brought us to a discovery of the *more* God has for us. Be encouraged to trust in the love of the One who can provide more than you'll need. Deep, passionate, fulfilling sexual experiences require a relationship between two people who've committed to trusting and loving one another within the context of marriage. It is the result of depth in all other aspects of life. Sex is a profound soul exchange, a giving and receiving that can only happen when we submit to God's plan—because that's how He created us. Fall in love with Christ and everything else will fall into place. I pray you won't settle for anything less.

APPLY TO LIFE

> Take a moment to write a letter to your spouse—whether you're currently single, married, engaged, dating, or not dating. Explain what you're feeling right now in terms of sex and sexuality. Write about your hopes and dreams, and also your fears.

> Regardless if marriage is in your future or even if you're already married, letter-writing is still a way you can become a more selfless, giving, God-honoring person. Consider writing the first of many letters to God. Tell Him what you're feeling now and how you'd like Him to work in your life.

END NOTES

SESSION 1

1. Rand Corporation, "A Worksite Parenting Program that Works: Research Highlights," 2011 [cited 1 June 2012]. Available from the Internet: *www.rand.org.*
2. Guttmacher Institute, "Facts on American Teens' Sexual and Reproductive Health," February 2012 [cited 1 June 2012]. Available from the Internet: *www.guttmacher.org.*
3. Kaiser Family Foundation, "Sex on TV 4, Report," November 2005 [cited 1 June 2012]. Available from the Internet: *kff.org.*

SESSION 2

1. holy. "Dictionary.com Unabridged" [cited 15 March 2012]. Available from the Internet: *dictionary.reference.com.*
2. honorable. "Dictionary.com Unabridged" [cited 16 March 2012]. Available from the Internet: *dictionary.reference.com.*
3. Matthew Henry, *Commentary on the Whole Bible Volume 1 (Genesis to Deuteronomy).* Available from the Internet: *www.ccel.org.*
4. I first heard this discussion of bridges in a marriage class at Southwestern Baptist Theological Seminary. It's based on the book *A Joyful Meeting* by Drs. Mike Grace and Joy Grace.
5. Satoshi Kanazawa, "Male Brain vs. Female Brain I: Why do Men Try to Figure Out Their Relationships? Why do Women Talk to Their Cars?," March 16, 2008 [cited 2 June 2012]. Available from the Internet: *www.psychologytoday.com.*

SESSION 3

1. Ysolt Usigan, "Top 10 most promiscuous cities in the U.S." 2012 [cited 1 June 2012]. Available from the Internet: *www.cbsnews.com.*
2. Demosthenes, from the oration "Against Neaera, Section 122" [cited 1 June 2012]. Available from the Internet: *www.perseus.tufts.edu.*
3. Lucius Annasus Seneca. *Moral Essays.* Translated by John W. Basore. The Loeb Classical Library. London: W. Heinemann,1928-1935. 3 vols.: Volume III [cited 1 June 2012]. Available from the Internet: *www.stoics.com.*
4. Daniel R. Heimbach, Ph.D., "Sexual Purity in a Hook-Up Culture," *Family North Carolina Magazine,* July/August 2007 [cited 1 June 2012]. Available from the Internet: *www.ncfamily.org.*
5. Frederick Buechner, *Godric: A Novel* (New York: HarperCollins, 1983), 153.
6. Victor C. Strasburger, MD, "Policy Statement: Sexuality, Contraception, and the Media," *Pediatrics Journal* August 3, 2010 [cited 1 June 2012]. Available from the Internet: *pediatrics.aappublications.org.*
7. For more information on this topic, see the chapter "Starving the Eyes" in *Every Man's Battle: Winning the War on Sexual Temptation One Victory at a Time* by Stephen Arterburn and Fred Stoeker with Mike Yorkey (Colorado Springs: WaterBrook Press, 2000).
8. Robert Weiss, *Untangling the Web* (New York: Alyson Publications, 2006), 41.
9. Sebastian Anthony, "Just how big are porn sites?" April 4, 2012 [cited 1 June 2012]. Available from the Internet: *www.extremetech.com.*

10. USLegal on Internet Law, "Pornography," 2010 [cited 1 June 2012]. Available from the Internet: *internetlaw.uslegal.com*.
11. Statistics from the *"Real Marriage* Research Brief," 2012 [cited 1 June 2012]. Available from the Internet: *www.pastormark.tv*
12. Ibid., *"Real Marriage* Research Brief."
13. Peter Kreeft, *Love is Stronger than Death* (San Francisco: Ignatius Press, 1992), 34.
14. to steward. Adapted from "Dictionary.com Unabridged" [cited 15 March 2012]. Available from the Internet: *dictionary.reference.com*.
15. Matt Carter and Halim Suh, *Creation Restored* (Nashville, TN: LifeWay Press, 2012), 43.
16. Elisabeth Elliot, *Passion and Purity* (Grand Rapids: Revell, 2006), 69.
17. Donna Freitas, *Sex and the Soul* (Oxford University Press, 2008), 153, 155.

SESSION 4

1. Marie E. Tomeo, et al., "Comparative Data of Childhood and Adolescence Molestation in Heterosexual and Homosexual Persons," Archives of Sexual Behavior 30 (2001): 539. As footnoted in *Getting It Straight*, Peter Sprigg and Timothy Dailey, eds., (Family Research Council, 2004), 140.
2. Watkins & Bentovim, "The Sexual Abuse of Male Children and Adolescents," 316. As footnoted in *Getting It Straight*, Peter Sprigg and Timothy Dailey, eds., (Family Research Council, 2004), 141.
3. JoAnn Hibbert Hamilton, "The Official Website of Citizens for Families," 2007-2011 [cited 1 June 2012]. Available from the Internet: *www.strengthenthefamily.net*.
4. Ibid., JoAnn Hibbert Hamilton.
5. Långström N, Rahman Q, Carlström E, Lichtenstein P (February 2010). "Genetic and environmental effects on same-sex sexual behavior: a population study of twins in Sweden." Arch Sex Behav 39 (1): 75–80.
6. Michael King, et al., "A systematic review of mental disorder, suicide, and deliberate self harm in lesbian, gay and bisexual people," *BMC Psychiatry*, August 18, 2008 [cited 1 June 2012]. Available from the Internet: *www.biomedcentral.com*.
7. Genevra Pittman, "Social environment linked to gay teen suicide risk," April 18, 2011 [cited 1 June 2012]. Available from the Internet: *www.reuters.com*.
8. J. Michael Bailey, Ph.D., "Homosexuality and Mental Illness," Archives of General Psychiatry, October 1999, 56(10):883-884 [cited 1 June 2012]. Available from the Internet: *archpsyc.ama-assn.org*.
9. OneNewsNow, "Study: Homosexual lifestyle strongly linked to depression, suicide," September 20, 2008 [cited 1 June 2012]. Available from the Internet: *www. onenewsnow.com*.
10. NPR Staff, "LGBTs Are 10% Of US Population? Wrong, Says Demographer," June 8, 2011 [cited 1 June 2012]. Available from the Internet: *www.npr.org*.
11. Stanton L. Jones and Mark A. Yarhouse, Homosexuality: The Use of Scientific Research in the Use of the Church's Moral Debate (Downey Grove, Illinois: InterVarsity Press, 2000), 31, 34-36.

12. Anjani Chandra, Ph.D., et al., "Sexual Behavior, Sexual Attraction, and Sexual Identity in the United States: Data From the 2006–2008 National Survey of Family Growth," *National Health Statistics Reports* Number 36, March 3, 2011 [cited 1 June 2012]. Available from the Internet: *www.cdc.gov*.

13. Ibid., Anjani Chandra.

14. Roger J. Magnuson, *Are Gay Rights Right?* (Portland: Multnomah Press, 1990), 43.

15. Nathaniel S. Lehrman, M.D., "Homosexuality: Some Neglected Considerations," *Journal of American Physicians and Surgeons* Volume 10, Number 3, Fall 2005.

16. NPR Staff, "LGBTs Are 10% Of US Population? Wrong, Says Demographer."

17. Magnuson, 57.

18. Dennis Prager, "Who supports same-sex marriage?" Jewish World Review, March 9, 2004 [cited 6 June 2012]. Available from the Internet: *www.jewishworldreview.com*.

19. Charles Krauthammer, "When John and Jim Say, 'I Do'" July 22 [cited 1 June 2012]. Available from the Internet: *www.cnn.com*.

20. Associated Press, "Text of President-elect Barack Obama's acceptance speech," November 5, 2008 [cited 1 June 2012]. Available from the Internet: *www.chron.com*.

21. Katelyn Polantz, "N.C. Marriage Vote Opponents Play on Civil Rights Message," May 8, 2012 [cited 1 June 2012]. Available from the Internet: *www.pbs.org*.

22. Ed Stetzer, "President Obama, Same-Sex Marriage, and the Future of Evangelical Response," May 10, 2012 [cited 1 June 2012]. Available from the Internet: *www. edstetzer.com*.

SESSION 5

1. Kathryn A. London, "Children of Divorce," Data From the National Vital Statistics System Series 21, No. 46., 1989 [cited 1 June 2012]. Available from the Internet: *www.cdc.gov*.

2. Lamar Clarkson, "Divorce rates falling, report finds," May 19, 2011 [cited 1 June 2012]. Available from the Internet: *articles.cnn.com*.

3. The American Academy of Child and Adolescent Psychiatry, "Child Sexual Abuse," March 2011 [cited 1 June 2012]. Available from the Internet: *aacap.org*.

4. Rape, Abuse, and Incest National Network, "Statistics," 2009 [cited 31 May 2012]. Available from the Internet: *www.rainn.org*.

5. The National Center for Victims of Crime, "Acquaintance Rape," [cited 31 May 2012]. Available from the Internet: *www.ncvc.org*.

6. Ibid., Rape, Abuse, and Incest National Network.

7. Justin Holcomb and Lindsey A. Holcomb, *Rid of My Disgrace: Hope and Healing for Victims of Sexual Assault* (Wheaton, IL: Crossway, 2011), 91.

8. Melva Thomas Johnson & Jesse Johnson, "Marital Affairs: A Harsh Reality," [cited 31 May 2012]. Available from the Internet: *mfgmarriage.com*.

9. R. C. Sproul, *The Holiness of God* (Carol Stream, IL: Tyndale, 2000), 159.

10. Adapted from Milton S. Magness, *Thirty Days to Hope & Freedom from Sexual Addiction: The Essential Guide to Beginning Recovery and Preventing Relapse* (Carefree, Arizona: Gentle Path Press, 2011), 179-183.

11. "How do I overcome the temptation to masturbate?" April 11, 2012 [cited 4 June 2012]. Available from the Internet: *focusonthefamily.com*.

SESSION 6

1. Rodney and Selma Wilson, "The secret to great sex" [cited 31 May 2012]. Available from the Internet: *www.lifeway.com*.

2. Steve Farrar, *Finishing Strong: Going the Distance for Your Family* (Sisters, Oregon: Multnomah Publishers, Inc., 1995), 84.

3. Harville Hendrix and Helen LaKelly Hunt, *Receiving Love: Transform Your Relationship By Letting Yourself Be Loved* (New York, NY: Atria Books, 2004), 17.

4. Larry Crabb, *The Marriage Builder: A Blueprint for Couples and Counselors* (Grand Rapids: Zondervan, 1992), 91.

5. Bruce Marshall, *The World, the Flesh, and Father Smith* (Boston: Houghton Mifflin Company, 1945), 108.

6. United States Census Bureau, "Number, Timing, and Duration of Marriages and Divorces: 2009," May 2011 [cited 31 May 2012]. Available from the Internet: *www.census.gov*.

7. Leigh Kramer, "The church needs a different view of sex & singleness," [cited 31 May 2012]. Available from the Internet: *goodwomenproject.com*.

8. Charles Stanley, *Our Unmet Needs* (Nashville, TN: Thomas Nelson, Inc., 1999), 53.

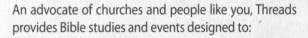

Threads

An advocate of churches and people like you, Threads provides Bible studies and events designed to:

cultivate community We need people we can call when the tire's flat or when we get the promotion. And it's those people—the day-in-day-out people—who we want to walk through life with and learn about God from.

provide depth Kiddie pools are for kids. We're looking to dive in, head first, to all the hard-to-talk-about topics, tough questions, and thought-provoking Scriptures. We think this is a good thing, because we're in process. We're becoming. And who we're becoming isn't shallow.

lift up responsibility We are committed to being responsible—doing the right things like recycling and volunteering. And we're also trying to grow in our understanding of what it means to share the gospel, serve the poor, love our neighbors, tithe, and make wise choices about our time, money, and relationships.

encourage connection We're looking for connection with our church, our community, with somebody who's willing to walk along side us and give us a little advice here and there. We'd like opportunities to pour our lives out for others because we're willing to do that walk-along-side thing for someone else, too. We have a lot to learn from people older and younger than us. From the body of Christ.

We're glad you picked up this study. Please come by and visit us at *threadsmedia.com*.

ALSO FROM THREADS . . .

CREATION UNRAVELED
THE GOSPEL ACCORDING TO GENESIS
BY MATT CARTER AND HALIM SUH

The words we read in Genesis are the same words that provided hope for hungry Israelites in the wilderness, breathed courage into the heart of David, and fed the soul of Jesus Himself during His time on earth. God's promises are as relevant today as they were "in the beginning."

Matt Carter serves as lead pastor of The Austin Stone Community Church in Austin, Texas. He and his wife, Jennifer, have three children.

Halim Suh and his wife, Angela, also have three kids. Halim is an elder and pastor of equipping at The Austin Stone Community Church.

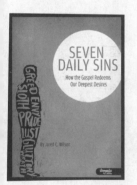

SEVEN DAILY SINS
HOW THE GOSPEL REDEEMS OUR DEEPEST DESIRES
BY JARED C. WILSON

The so-called "seven deadly sins"—lust, greed, envy, sloth, pride, gluttony, wrath—are not merely things we "do," but as Jesus reveals, conditions of our heart. Even if we don't act on them, we carry these desires around every day. How does the gospel address the needs at the root of these sins and empower us to break patterns of bondage to them? *Seven Daily Sins* reveals from Scripture how Christians can experience freedom by the redemptive power of the gospel of Jesus.

Jared C. Wilson is the author of several books, including Gospel Wakefulness *and* Your Jesus Is Too Safe: Outgrowing a Drive-Thru, Feel-Good Savior. *He's the pastor of Middletown Church in Middletown Springs, Vermont. Visit him online at jaredcwilson.com.*

MENTOR
HOW ALONG-THE-WAY DISCIPLESHIP WILL CHANGE YOUR LIFE
BY CHUCK LAWLESS

Drawing from biblical examples like Jesus and His disciples and Paul and Timothy, author Chuck Lawless explores the life-transforming process of a mentoring relationship. This study is both a practical and spiritual guide to biblical mentoring, providing easy-to-model life application for how to have and be a mentor.

Chuck Lawless is vice president for Global Theological Advance of the International Mission Board. He's the author of several books, including Spiritual Warfare: Biblical Truth for Victory, Discipled Warriors, *and* Putting on the Armor. *Dr. Lawless is also president of the Lawless Group, a church consulting firm (thelawlessgroup.com).*

threadsmedia.com/store 1.800.458.2772 LifeWay Christian Stores

FOR FULL DETAILS ON ALL OF THREADS' STUDIES, VISIT *THREADSMEDIA.COM.*